THERE IS AN i IN TEAM

HOW TO GET **REAL TEAM RESULTS** INSTEAD OF REAL BAD TEAMS PRETENDING TO GET RESULTS

JACK LYNCH

There is an I in Team
Copyright © 2025 by Jack Lynch.

For information contact: info@owlpenguin.net
http://www.OwlPenguin.net

Cover and interior formatting by KUHN Design Group | kuhndesigngroup.com

ISBN: 979-8-9994454-1-4 (paperback)
ISBN: 979-8-9994454-0-7 (eBook)
Library of Congress Control Number: 2025914768

First Edition: September 2025

I would like to thank all the organizations, people, droids, teams, supervisors, managers, directors, human foliage, vice presidents, executive vice presidents, people with really bizarre titles, and CEOs I have worked with and for, and who have worked for me over the years.

All of you were an inspiration. I will leave it to each of you to determine if I used your abilities as an example of great performance or my inspiration to write about what not to do...ever

CONTENTS

CHAPTER 1

WELCOME TO TEAMWORK

"It is far better to be alone, than to be in bad company."

GEORGE WASHINGTON

Would you like a dollar for every time you've heard about the importance of Teamwork? It is the universal truth, the Holy Grail, the epitome of all things good with the world of business. Corporations and governments have spent millions of dollars in team training and so-called "organizational analysis" to foster teamwork—and that was just to pay the consultants.

Consider the millions of dollars in opportunity costs of having your employees be in training as opposed to doing their "day job," which is helping your team prosper. Why do we spend this amount of time, money, and energy? It is all in the noble pursuit of a magical potion, the elixir that will enable us to become more innovate, double our productivity, and of course, dominate our competition. One drink will create high-octane teams producing results in geometric proportion to the number of people on the team.

Yet, after all the team research, training, books, videos, motivational speeches, and millions of dollars in becoming a "destination workplace" to attract these amazing team members, what are the results? Organizations are still struggling with failed strategic plans, poorly executed projects, and dysfunctional teams while members of the "team" point fingers and executives wonder what has gone wrong with their amazing strategic vision. In more than thirty years of business experience managing people, multimillion-dollar projects, large business units, and departments, as well as being a part of cross-functional teams, I have seen all types of teams. Teams that jumped over bars that everyone thought were unattainable and teams that couldn't jump over the bar if you placed it on the ground and offered to carry them over it.

Why the disparity? The simple truth is that a nebulous "team" doesn't create results. The quality of your individual performers on the team is what brings long-term sustainable results. It is time to face the fallacies of the herd mentality touting the greatness of teamwork as opposed to individual greatness that comes together to create great team results. When you have a team of great individuals you can then create great organizations that achieve success working toward a shared objective. Only then will you be able to move your organization to the next level of successful performance—before your competitor. Simple concept? Yes it is. Applied in organizations? Not so much.

It's easy to see why. Everywhere in popular culture the magical power of teamwork is lauded. What sports team doesn't respond to a question about how they won with the canned answer—it was a team effort. Even when a team loses a game is it because one person dropped a pass or struck out? No, the answer is, "We didn't come together as a team. Coaches and players all have to accept responsibility." The problem is that after years of being force-fed this propaganda as a society, we are starting to believe it. As if all we need to do is hire a team facilitator consultant and a 0 and 16 football team will go to the Super Bowl. Even more ridiculous is thinking that adding a performance monitoring database will take a last place baseball team to the World Series. In reality what works is creating realistic financial and operational objectives, and then building your leadership and teams around high-performing individuals. This is what drastically turns a team around—not team training or myriad programs to improve employee engagement.

This love of the team concept has been magnified as organizations fooled themselves into thinking many of the productivity gains realized were the result of all their amazing "team efforts." In reality the tremendous productivity gains derived in recent years have been achieved through application of technology that covered up some incredibly defective organizational structures, practices, processes, and yes, people. The application of technology over the years—from word processors, spreadsheets, and email, to applications automating manual processes—enabled organizations to reduce or completely eliminate entire job classifications. This included things such as clerical work for data entry, factory assembly line work, and the collection and storage of data.

This trend is continuing as the use of technology in the collection, mining, and use of data is now permeating our entire society. Recent advances in machine learning, now incorporated into the umbrella of Artificial Intelligence, is continuing the trend of integrating technology into every fabric of society. In theory having the data at our fingertips is supposed to help us make better decisions. The jury is still out on how many of these numerous technology and data sets are really helping your team members better understand how to solve the challenges facing your organization as opposed to adding new technology that generates more problems to solve.

As it pertains to productivity, technology is the blunt-force instrument that has enabled exponential improvements, not your brilliant team-building training program or application of some repackaged fad management theory. No matter how bad your processes, people, or strategies are, you could make gains in productivity through the brute-force application of technology. While the thousands of people with a vested interest in selling and consulting on process improvement and technology may disagree, we are entering a new era where any business can buy technology that could potentially produce quantifiable productivity savings and maybe better customer "experiences." The key words in the preceding sentence are potential, maybe, and quantifiable. Rare is the organization that honestly validates what happened after the improvement initiative was completed as opposed to what was on the sales presentation or board slide.

As technology becomes more and more embedded into how organizations operate, the organizational and process weakness in companies will become more apparent in the coming years. The preceding statement should be qualified. Organizational and process weakness will become apparent to the people who do the work on your team. Whether you understand and act is an entirely different matter. Investing millions in precious capital on the generic word "technology" to make poor teams better typically brings unintended consequences. Did you reduce operating cost or did you only transfer cost from one team and enabled another department to add additional enterprise support infrastructure with ever-increasing budgets? Maybe you enabled one area to show productivity gains while ignoring the cost of adding additional technology infrastructure, support for complicated tools, consulting services, and hiring support employees at higher cost. When that fails you also have the opportunity to cover your failed initiatives while still claiming technology process improvements and great leadership. Or you simply outsource core business functions to entities using an allegedly sophisticated reduced cost model. This cost model, otherwise known as "outsourcing human capital," enables you to send what your internal communications claims is your organization's most important asset to low-cost areas of the world that have a different idea of workforce management.

Before the software developers and other technologists reach for their communication devices to post their disagreement, I am not talking about how the application of technology will continue to drive automation of various operational tasks, new products and services, or the incredible advances in medicine and science. This is directed against the fallacy of assuming the advances in technology translate into advances in human interaction as it pertains to communication and teamwork to get real results by leveraging technology. Most team leaders react to problems by relying on personal experience solving what they perceive as similar situations in the past. If the organizational challenges are different or significantly more difficult there is a tendency to look for technology solutions to save the day before understanding the poorly constructed foundation of the team that is blocking success. It is much easier just to regurgitate what they read, hear from companies selling solution, and what they see from those amazing colorful slides provided by consultants on how the application of the latest technology will lead to the promised land. The arms race will continue as companies pour more resources and capital into technology for expensive software applications that will allegedly provide the golden ticket to exponential service improvement, great products, and customer relationships.

TEAMWORK MOMENT OF TRUTH

The application of technology has the power to help a team become more successful while also creating the illusion that all members of the team are creating this success.

The problem is most organizations are buying similar technology at this point. Instead of accepting this conventional wisdom, ask yourself: What is the improvement that technology brings to your team? If your answer is, we automated a process, you are well on your way to sinking money down an automation rat hole to generate poor results. That statement isn't entirely accurate. Automation usually takes a team that doesn't work together, or in the business buzzword word of the day "collaborate," and speeds up all their dysfunctional processes. The good news is you will have plenty of workflow diagrams to show your alleged collaboration processes to the auditors. If your answer is to leverage technology to collect data that will help provide insights to give your team a competitive edge and/ or develop new solutions for the market, then at least you are on the right track. You might already have spent millions of dollars on securing the data and have the ability to produce thousands of pages of reports and colorful graphs. The real question is: Do you have the right people who can do anything with the information? Can your team work together, connect the dots, and translate the information into success? Many say, few do.

Increasing productivity and teamwork through automation also tends to create an internal focus that deviates attention from the key components of a successful organization: the people paying the bills, i.e., customers and owners. Nothing says we want your business like the statement; "Your call is important to us. Due to unusually heavy call volumes every time you call 24x7 365 days a year your hold time is now 60 minutes. Try calling us on Wednesday at 2:00AM for faster service." It's great that due to technology advancements, instead of saying please stay on the line for the next available agent we can now tell our customers how long it will take to answer the call or call you back when it is more convenient for us to answer your question. Another great thing is to tell them if they don't have time to wait on hold for one hour, they can consult your knowledge base. Yes, the knowledge base they already looked at that didn't answer their question or your AI chat bot with the friendly picture that keeps popping up and offering to help, which didn't solve their problem either.

While my observations regarding current leadership and popular theories will appear to some to be cynical and pessimistic, I prefer to view them as cynically optimistic. One must first face the reality of the current situation in order to create positive change for the future. It is cynical in expecting most so-called leaders will implement change on their own as opposed to faux change to show they improved the team. Yet it is optimistic in that a few leaders will rise above the rest and show the way to truly create high-performing teams delivering real results. Even one team leader can be an outpost of competency in a sea of mediocrity, thus enabling others to take notice and possibly emulate.

The ideas expressed in this book are based on a lifetime of experience working on teams, consulting with various organizations, service roles, technical positions, leading large projects, managing people, and senior leadership positions. At my first job as a bus boy in my teens, my manager Bobby held a team meeting. In between yelling at us about super important things like not wiping down counters the correct way when we were not busy, he stated something that stayed with me all these years, "Everything you learn working here will apply to everything you do for the rest of your working life." Cleaning tables, pouring water into glasses, and dealing with the crazy people I work with and customers can be applied to every job I will ever have in my life? That statement confirmed this crazy, psychotic restaurant manager was an idiot. I couldn't wait until I had a big-boy job someday instead of bus boy.

Soon I was able to get my wish and "someday" arrived. My experience working with teams progressed from bus boy to waiter to cook. Then I was fortunate to work in one-hundred-degree heat in a unionized metal foundry and then on a team as a carpenter assistant building condos. There was also the time when I became a leader of a different type of team, a local rock band. This was followed by moving into technology when I worked on large computer and communication systems. My journey continued into service sales and account management roles, project management of various large implementations, managing progressively larger work teams, and finally senior leadership positions managing multimillion-dollar P&Ls and leading a company subsidiary.

While the concepts I discuss in this book were forged by my work experiences and the people I worked with, they were also influenced by my on-going love of continuous learning. My family instilled in me the value of life-long learning and education, for which I will be forever grateful. They also believed that college was the only way to get an education and be successful. I think it is inspiring when people talk about the many obstacles they overcame to be the first person in their family to go to college. I took a different track. I became the only person on either side of the family born after 1900 to drop out of college. My parents, both my grandfathers who were university department heads, and my grandmothers, who also excelled in college, were not amused.

While my education took a different route it did not stop. The importance of education continued through reading, listening to the life stories of others, and the real-world experience of working with a variety of people from diverse backgrounds and experiences. These were all important teachers outside of the academic lens on how to solve problems and be a leader of teams. One of the key fundamentals I learned was appreciating the people on the team who were responsible for the success of the team.

TEAMWORK MOMENT OF TRUTH

The leadership style of a team leader may be different, but if you don't respect the individual contributors on your team, you are on the journey called team failure.

I also learned about leaders who thought they should command respect and be followed just because they were the boss, had a title, and any number of formal degrees and certifications. One of these was usually a Certificate of Insanity. None of those things translates into the skills required to be a great team leader.

Your job as a leader is to establish a culture of excellence for your team to achieve the goals that are set for it. You must also support a culture that fosters a climate of trust on the team and provides opportunities for growth. To create and sustain this culture you must engage with your team and be empathetic about the challenges they face and make the appropriate changes when required. This includes making difficult decisions and removing obstacles such as removing any team members who are not contributing to the mission. There is no magic potion, methodology, or roadmap that makes any of this easy.

During my journey I have made many mistakes, experienced personal and team failures, worked on great teams, and of course worked on teams that failed no matter the efforts of good people on the team. Learning from failure, while difficult and humbling, is an important part of any team leader's journey. Along the way I also returned to formal education and earned some of those pieces of parchment my parents and grandparents believed were so important. However, one important lesson getting those pieces of paper did teach me was how little they help in becoming a great leader. You get only what you put into the effort to learn and grow. Notice I didn't say it wasn't important to wave those pieces of paper around at Ye Olde Team Human Resource Door when you inquire about a leadership role. There is no question that those papers enable you to more easily overcome the fictious barrier constructed by organizations if you want to eventually have the opportunity to be a team leader.

After acquiring all this knowledge and experience I realized that Bobby was right, at least about working on teams. At his restaurant I learned about good and bad leadership characteristics. I learned how great individuals can overcome poor leadership and team members. I witnessed how some teams worked well and others failed spectacularly even when using the same tools and processes. I also learned what happens when a so-called leader just presses the "Easy Button" instead of addressing the root cause of a problem. It was also an education to be a part of a diverse group of humans who were placed in a team environment to achieve a goal and how unpredictable the outcomes are in spite of how much effort you put into it.

The same principles of effective leadership and building strong teams are evident regardless of whether in a restaurant, rock band, factory, computer manufacturer, financial institution, small software development company, a not-for-profit company, a large fortune 100 company, or even a small volunteer community club. Our challenge is resisting the temptation of thinking there is a shortcut, a magic bullet, some software application, training program, or consultant engagement that will lead us to the promised land of creating a successful team. The other challenge is thinking that you're the smartest person in the room and know everything about how to make the team successful. No, you are not and no you don't.

TEAMWORK MOMENT OF TRUTH

When someone offers you a magic bullet to fix your team's problems the only thing you are usually fixing is adding revenue to their balance sheet.

While the focus of this book is directed to those in team leadership roles, organizational team incompetence is both a top-down and bottom-up problem. If you claim you can't make any improvements in your department or yourself because you don't have "buy-in" from your executive team or support from your manager, I suggest you are part of the problem. Consider the preceding statement tough love. No matter where you are in an organization you can begin improving it today once you realize you have the ability to achieve success over what you control through your individual effort. Leadership by doing is a powerful force that will influence others both above and below to begin the process in their own organizations. Remember, even if you find your efforts to improve the team are blocked by an organizational culture of complacency, cluelessness, and/or incompetency, there is still hope for you. The skills you build in your attempt to create a high-performing team can be used to move on to another team that will genuinely appreciate your contribution to creating success.

Now, go TEAM!!!!

CHAPTER 2

THE SYNERGISTIC TEAM CONCEPT

1 + 1 DOES NOT EQUAL 3

"To follow by faith alone is to follow blindly."

BENJAMIN FRANKLIN

have a confession to make. It's about a dark secret I've hidden for years through hundreds of presentations, business books, and management meetings. I despise one of the most popular buzz words in organizational team history: Synergy. This evil concept has wasted more time and effort in organizational analysis than any other fake buzzword. The first thing to do is to eliminate "Synergy" from your vocabulary as a fix to your team problems before we go any further on outlining both the huge obstacles for success followed by the path to success. I use the term "new" only in the context of our current society attention span. The path to success is more like an ancient scroll discovered in a cave by the Dead Sea. This scroll contains the secret of universal team success that had been lost. During this lost period team mystics who teach team "collaboration" at universities and the dark arts of business consulting have grown in influence.

My initial encounter with synergy occurred many years ago

in my first position as a manager. No longer "just" a technician working on computer systems, I had joined the ranks of management. This happened soon after my company was acquired by a small startup firm created over one hundred years ago by a gentleman named Alexander Graham Bell. It was now time to receive one of the many lessons they do not teach in business management school. After the acquisition, or should the statement be due to the acquisition, one of my new accounts was very unhappy with service levels and demanded a meeting with our senior service management executives.

The director called a meeting to discuss meeting strategies, develop charts, and create a stunning presentation. As a new member of the service management team, I didn't know what to expect. The good news was my boss was very confident we had a plan and assured me this would get worked out. We met our Vice President at the hotel the night before the client presentation. It was inspiring to see my director and VP develop the "meeting strategy" on how they would handle the client. It was obvious they knew what they were doing.

The day of the meeting we arrived at the customer location and were escorted into a conference room. We sat on one side of a very large conference table and waited. After ten minutes the client vice president arrived with his entourage. They did not look friendly. My Vice President began the presentation thanking our client and explaining how our new combined organization would provide synergistic value to our customers. Now that sounded impressive! The client said nothing and just glared at us as we moved along from colorful presentation slide to slide until the following slide appeared on the screen:

> ## We have created Synergy that will bring you more value!

The client vice president stopped us and just repeated the word, "Synergy? Synergy?" He then paused, stared at my boss for what seemed like an eternity, and jumped out of his chair throwing his copy of the presentation across the table. "Synergy?" he shouted, "THERE IS NO FLUFFY SYNERGY. I don't want to hear about fluffy synergy; I want you to fix your fluffy service problems now or you're fluffing fired!" Actually, he didn't really yell "fluffy you" at us numerous times. This is just an attempt to keep the story family rated. The most impressive part was the client's ability to use the word fluffy as a noun, verb, adjective, adverb, conjunction, and dangling particle in a thirty-second run-on sentence without taking a breath.

My synergy-spouting leaders were speechless. They went from displaying "synergy" to the tried-and-true business management practice perfected over four thousand years. They groveled and begged for another chance, including offering a price concession. The client said he would give us one more chance and walked out of the room. On the ride back my management "team" performed another important management technique: delegation. My director snapped, "We don't care how you do it, fix it or look for another job." So much for Management Team Synergy

If you do nothing else after reading this book stop using the word Synergy to impress people with what your team will do. Synergy is an evil business buzzword that maintains the theory that a team can achieve more than the sum of its parts. If a corporation gained one dollar for every time an executive or manager uttered "synergy," profits would increase three-fold. Alas this is not the case. In fact, the opposite appears to be true. The amount of team synergy produced is inversely proportional to the number of times an executive or manager utters the word.

There are two theories as to why mentioning team synergy hasn't produced the gains it is credited with.

> **Theory 1:** It was concocted by people who fail to appreciate the physics of the known universe.

> **Theory 2:** It was developed by consultants concocting a "new" methodology to sell desperate people looking for a quick fix to their typically self-created problems.

Both are very valid theories. First, we will explore theory one, which states synergy was concocted by people who fail to appreciate the physics of the known universe. If we view this statement as a scientific theory, we can postulate that if you have three people, each of whom produces three units of work, and have them now work as a team you will get more value than with each person working separately.

As they say in the scientific community—let's study this phenomenon. For the purpose of this "experiment" let us postulate the following:

First, we'll set a baseline for the average number of work units an employee provides an organization. Yes, there will be math involved as we explore this highly complicated algorithm, so get ready to exercise your brain.

Typical Team Member Work Units Formula:

1 Employee = 3 work units

3 Employees * 3 work units = 9 work units

Now we will look at a team that has applied the magic Synergy elixir:

High Performing Synergistic Team Formula:

3 Employees x 3 work units = 9 work units + SPV = 12 work units

SPV = Synergistic Performance Value as calculated by:

$$(\Delta S = Q / T + niN) + (e\text{-}Ei/kBT\sum ie\text{-}Ei/kBT) = 3 \ SPV$$

If you compare the two groups one will produce nine work units and the other will produce an incredible twelve units of work with the same group of people. This is like the cold fusion theory of providing cheap power. If we can just add an undefinable variable to the equation, we can solve for X and have more power than we know what to do with. Incredible yet highly unlikely.

The good news is there is a mathematical way to describe the likely outcome of teams assembled today. Here is how the equation works in the real world, and yes, I have personally seen the testing results with hundreds of teams. You put together a team to complete a project. With "3" representing the average work effort of an employee, the team consists of the following employees who produce the following work output on a day-to-day basis.

---

*. Important note on the above formula for normal dolts who did not receive a Ph.D. in mathematics: There is a complex mathematical algorithm and sophisticated modeling tool behind the formula; however, it is far too complex for people with normal intelligence to grasp. Since you are reading it in a book, treat it like other computer models and theories sited by "experts," the media, and anonymous internet commentators as proof in support of whatever argument is being made. In other words, just believe it must be true because it fits your beliefs.

Real World Team Performance:
Employee A = 4 work units
Employee B = 2 work units
Employee C = 0.5 work units (when they bother to show
   up at all)

Now do the math: 4 + 2 + 0.5 = 6.5 work units. Voila, a decrease in productively! And this is a best-case scenario. In real-world team situations Employee A, who was doing four work units sees that everyone is getting credit as a "team" while she does all the work and thus decreases her output. Now the formula becomes 3+2+0.5 = 5.5

Congratulations, you have taken a standard work output of nine, reduced this to 6.5 by making it a team project, and then moved it to 5.5 by putting your workers on a synergistic "team"…Nice job!

I call the decrease that comes from team formation Dysynergy. There is only one thing you proved on this project. It is a "syn" you spent all this energy and didn't get the results you were looking for. How do you avoid Dysynergy? How do you achieve real productivity gains? If you answered put people through team-builder training you have followed in the footsteps of thousands of managers who just want to wish their problems away and convince themselves they are fixing the problem, or at least convince their CEO they are fixing their "team problem." If you really want to further decrease the productivity of the team used in the example, follow the training with an off-site team-builder event. In addition to losing an additional day of work output, the team will hate each other even more because they had to fake a positive attitude and demonstrate cooperation through the entire workshop.

Another, more effective management approach comes to mind

to solve this particular case study. Instead of hunting for the elusive endangered species known as the synergistic team, you would have been better off firing two members of the "team" and giving the remaining member a bonus if they increased their work output by one. Now that's what I call real Synergy. We will explore this concept in later chapters.

Are you still excited about the possibilities of creating synergistic cross-functional teams? Consider the Dysynergy teamwork output formula the next time some consultant gives you a fifty-page PowerPoint presentation with bountiful colors explaining how adding their "new" and expensive business execution modules will create synergistic motion in your organization! There is also the extensive and expensive team training you can put dysfunctional employees through, and which will reap tremendous benefits—at least to the consultant "coach." Of course, how can you put a price on the incredible productivity gains you will derive from a great color slide presentation?

TEAMWORK MOMENT OF TRUTH

Sometimes instead of attempting to improve team execution you should just execute the team.

You don't form a team just to form a team because everyone knows that teams get more done. *You form a team to complete a project that requires the skills identified as necessary to complete the tasks on the project.* This should appear to be the most self-evident sentence in the history of organizational behavior. Unfortunately, in the real world it is incredible to view the number of boat anchors, i.e., "team members," tied to teams yet organizations are unwilling to cut them free.

Now it is time to examine Theory Two. Have consultants generated an incredible amount of revenue with team training, books, and seminars on synergetic teams? There appears to be volumes of evidence supporting this theory, including your team synergy consultant's new 50-foot cabin cruiser. This is not to suggest that all consultants proposing you implement their program with expensive certification requirements are just trying to extract money from your business and placing it in theirs. You should just consider this could be a possibility.

The truth is out. There is no such thing as Synergy. It is a word made up to extract dollars from your budget by a consultant or by someone on your staff pretending to fix a problem. Attempting to train people to achieve this mythical state of performance is a drain on resources that could be better applied addressing real problems such as low-performer team member #3. I have yet to see any evidence of hard dollar savings over a period of time which results from training people to work on synergistic teams. Certainly, I've seen testimonials from consultants and managers justifying the training expense about how team productivity improvements were made. These testimonials from clients can be filed under "We just believe it must be helping because, well, we don't really have any other ideas, and the boss told us to fix a team problem."

TEAMWORK MOMENT OF TRUTH

It is a Syn to waste money and energy on trying to prove a theory that doesn't help your team succeed.

Before you throw your hands up in despair that you will never achieve synergy team nirvana, all is not lost. The point of this exercise is not to take away from the exciting possibilities of teamwork or the benefits to people who work on great teams. It is to highlight the dangers of running those team classes in a dysfunctional work area with poor leadership and wondering why LESS is being accomplished after you pay for the training.

Another reason that many organizations fall prey to this synergy junk science is that executives, in their rush to compete in the marketplace, have a clouded vision about their own organization's business maturity level. There is also a possibility that this may be due to a clouded vision of a team leader's own knowledge and business maturity. In upcoming chapters, we will explore the possibilities of how a lack of knowledge, maturity, mental stability, or any combination of these reasons could potentially play a role in overall team performance.

CEOs want to believe their direct reports and organizational structure support the goals of the company. Since this belief, bordering on denial, is extremely strong it makes sense that the addition of the magical silver bullet of team training and collaboration applications will enable them to leap into the next level of productivity gains and achieve the results they are looking for by building synergistic teams. The actual results are at best the same or typically two steps back. Your goal, no matter where you are in the organization, is to realistically measure where your organization is, accept where it is, and then take the steps necessary to move your "team" to the next level. Not wish your way into it with synergy.

I learned some valuable lessons from that synergistic meeting and from participating on many alleged synergistic teams.

1. BS Executive Presentations about synergistic teams only work if your client isn't looking for measurable results—even when given by polished acronym-spewing executives.

2. At the end of the day, no matter what the theory, process model, strategy, or team you choose to employ, your boss will just tell you to fix the problem.

3. There is a higher mathematical probability of Dysynergy results when a team is formed unless serious consideration is given to the actual skills required and the capability of the team members selected.

By the way, the customer was right: Our team had no Fluffy Synergy! Do you really have any?

CHAPTER 3

THE OBSTACLES TO SUCCESS

"Success is to be measured not so much by the position that one has reached in life... as by the obstacles which he has overcome while trying to succeed."

BOOKER T. WASHINGTON

There have been many studies conducted, some for extremely high billable dollar amounts, which sought to determine the obstacles to success for an organization. Reading this book will save you hundreds of hours of study and millions of dollars in consulting fees. How? All team obstacles to success have can be condensed into five easy-to-understand components:

1. Human Nature.
2. Your Executive Team.
3. Your Boss.
4. Your Employees.
5. You.

Perhaps you noticed that lack of teamwork was not on the list. This may be time for another Teamwork Moment of Truth:

TEAMWORK MOMENT OF TRUTH

Lack of teamwork is a symptom of a dysfunctional organization, not the reason for organizational failure.

As we explore each of these obstacles recognize that it doesn't matter how far back in time you go or how complex our world appears to be. You can attribute lack of teamwork and organizational failure to one or more of these five areas. This chapter is not for the faint of heart. Once you identify the degree to which each area creates havoc, instead of attempting to address the problem(s) you may instead just seek therapy. Before you attempt to fix any organizational problems, including a lack of teamwork, you must first understand how powerful these obstacles are. Recognize they can't be wished away by executive order, slogans, internal marketing, or a management training seminar, even if you can't bring yourself to say this to the boss. Of course, if the issue is Number #3, Your Boss, you must balance your desire to pay the mortgage with the potential reaction to sharing your analysis with her.

HUMAN NATURE

We spend an incredible amount of time and money determining how to make teams work better. While technology has made rapid advancements over the last 120 years it is safe to say that human nature has not evolved at the same pace. In fact, a brief tour of history shows that humans have been consistent for at least 5,000 years of recorded history. There have been good people and bad, hard workers and lazy workers, smart people and dumb people. In some instances, it is a combo meal of bad, lazy, and dumb people working for you. There is also a great deal of evidence that the percentage of sociopaths and a variety of lunatics in society has not decreased either. In turn this creates both well-run and poorly-run teams.

There is also nothing unique or complex about teamwork. As surprising as this may be to some, humans have always formed into teams to achieve common goals. Even more surprising: They also did it without consultants. The human nature response of what's in it for me determines the success of a team. There is a simple formula that has worked whether it was a hunting party 4,000 years ago, Genghis Khan's army in 1221, or a software development team today:

- Individuals work when they are motivated.
- Teams work when the individual team members work.
- Lack of individual performance on a team carries consequences.
- Lack of individual consequences reduces team performance.

While the tools of today are more complex, we as a species are no more complex than humans thousands of years ago. We have acquired vast knowledge about "things" and how the physical world works. We also laugh about how ignorant humans were in the dark ages. Two hundred and fifty years ago when a person was sick an "expert" in medicine administered a variety of treatments to cure them. Some treatments were less harmful than others. If a person didn't improve the medical consultant, aka doctor, proceeded to bleed the patient. At what point do you realize that bleeding a sick person makes them worse? Apparently, it took humans a couple of hundred years to figure out this is a bad medical "Best Practice."

Yet, this is exactly what we do in organizations. When an organization is sick, we first perform all sorts of treatments including team training. When that doesn't work and things get worse, we start to bleed it indiscriminately as opposed to targeting the disease causing the problem. Just like in 1743, sometimes the patient lives and we congratulate ourselves on bleeding them close to death. When the patient dies there was no correlation to the bleeding treatment used. It was just meant to be.

What drives us as humans—our motivations, our emotions, our mental capacity—has not changed. We just know more about our environment and how to build complicated tools. One only needs to observe humans in various areas of the world to see this to be true. There is a subset of people that maintains a work ethic. There is another subset that has a work ethic and is goal oriented. There is also a subset that does not have a work ethic and is motivated by the goal of doing as little productive work as possible. Achieving the goals of any team they are associated with doesn't make the top ten list of their individual goal objectives.

If you believe that all people want to do the best they can or will be motivated by working as a team to achieve a goal you need a human nature intervention. While there are ways to improve performance through a variety of incentives there is the law of diminishing returns. In some cases, there is the law of no returns on humans even if you promised them a golden palace if they reached a goal. They will just refuse to do it. Unfortunately, due to years of neglect, we have organizations that are full of these types of characters. Then we have the eternal human behavior optimist who believes in the proverb, "Teach a man to fish and he will feed himself for a lifetime." The reality is that some people are taught to fish. The challenge is getting them to fish if they can convince you into believing they deserve your fish for free. After all, fishing is hard.

Humans have varying degrees of talents, intellect, motivation to succeed, and physical abilities. Some people have a substantial talent. It is just the wrong talent for your team. Let's say I'm on a professional football team. No matter how dedicated I am to the team, easy to work with, and open for improvement, should I be on the team? Let me save you some time: I would be an "obstacle to success" in the team's effort to attain a championship. If you decided to incent the team and told me you would give me one million dollars if I could return a kick-off for a touchdown, what would be the results? Permanent injury to several vital parts of my body comes to mind, suffered from blunt force trauma but with zero yards to show for it. That would be the best case if I were able to maintain consciousness. Now, if you send me to a one-week seminar on improving my kick-off return skills taught by a world-renowned expert what would be the result? Permanent injury two seconds later than the first time. Your process team can now bank that as a 200% productivity improvement.

No amount of money, practice, or believing in the team will enable me to play in the National Football League. Yet, if an NFL team were a typical company team, nobody would be replaced no matter how bad it got. After people quit showing up to watch the game, we would then lay off 10% of the defensive team, enabling us to show a profit that year. Think about that after a consultant says they will "train" your people to work better together. Then ask yourself, can they be trained and if so, do they care to be trained?

It is also human nature to be unpredictable. Put the same human in the same situation fifty times and you will get the same result. Put them in the same situation the fifty-first time and you may get a different result. The human mind is an amazing device. The chemical reactions that fire a synapse are not as predictable as we think. Every time someone tries to bottle a methodology that appears to work well with team X and team Y, it turns into a disaster on team Z. The reason isn't training, executive buy-in, or the weather. The reason is human nature. Therefore, everything you do is an art form, with some general concepts and guidelines you can learn to help you achieve a goal. Creating a great team is never a math formula that can be replicated with the same components. Give the exact same musical instruments and training to two different orchestras and you will get two completely different results. Recognize this, accept it, and remember it when you are putting your team together.

YOUR EXECUTIVE TEAM

The executive team should be responsible for guiding the ship through good times and bad. The reason I say "should" is because the same reasons work teams fail can also be applied to executive teams. The facade of teamwork is present because everyone knows you have to say it, yet the same human nature factors still apply at the executive level. Unfortunately, poor decisions and flawed character traits in executives can significantly impact the overall organizational performance to a greater extent than one bad actor performing work on a project team. If you are an executive and think you are above the dysfunctional fray below you, read no further. We have just discovered a key contributor to your organization's problem. You're welcome.

The other issue is that some qualities in human nature such as ambition and egocentric behaviors are usually much stronger in people who have climbed to the top of any organization. Since most of these people worked in organizations where there weren't strong metrics or accountability, the building of fiefdoms through networking, smoke and mirrors, self-promotion, backstabbing, and political assassinations were important skill sets to learn. Pursuit of control and satisfaction of personal needs all come ahead of good organizational behavior.

Remember, an executive is a team leader on steroids. This is a problem if a new CEO decides to change course and bring accountability and true metrics into the organization. The executive team either never learned or forgot those tools due to lack of use. Some have the ability if motivated properly; however, most will continue to behave the same way. They will just assume this is another CEO initiative, pretend to support it knowing that it will pass, and soon it will be back to business as usual. Others will move on to other organizations voluntarily or involuntarily. The good news for you is that your dysfunctional competitor will pick them up due to the impressive titles and 'accomplishments' on their resume.

The problem is separating personal like from effectiveness. Ask each of them and they will say they support the strategies of the company and work as a team. If you don't have good metrics in place, or worse have them and don't demonstrate you are holding your executive team accountable, you have lost the battle to bring teamwork to your organization.

YOUR MANAGER, AKA THE BOSS

What is a manager? Despite what many HR departments and companies claim, most managers are in their positions because:

- They were a manager somewhere else and convinced you they were successful. Notice I didn't say they were successful.

- They have the "right" pedigree, e.g., degree, elite school, and/or certifications.

- The recruiter and hiring manager loved their dynamic, positive personality.

- They have perceived technical abilities they developed in a non-management role.

- They network well with executives.

- They just hung around the organization long enough to have the next-level title bestowed upon them.

Does any of this translate into being an effective manager? Ask yourself: Why do many people claim they want to be a manager? Is it because they have leadership abilities and skills to guide a team towards achieving the strategies and goals of the organization? While this is what is said in the interview, a case can be made there are other hidden motivations including: more money, ambition, status, or the desire to be a boss, i.e., control people. Do any of these qualities translate into effective team management? If you answered yes, I have a question for you. Did your boss order you to read this book? If the answer is yes, do you have any idea why?

Organizations are already behind the curve because their management staff is chock full of people there for the "promotion," ambition, control issues, or were perceived to be good at a previous non-management position. I say perceived since many organizations do not have the metrics in place that truly distinguish the ordinary or even poor from the extraordinary performer. If the management team is full of self-aggrandizing employees, do you think they are going to play nice together in the team management sandbox? Do you think you are gaining anything by putting these people into teams or management?

Here's a question you answer with a resounding "no." Do you think your employees are motivated to work together when you talk about teamwork when they see the daily antics of their team "boss" in action? This is not to say that all managers fall into this category. There are many great team managers who have ambition, work hard, and are motivated to succeed. My point is to knock some sense into those who believe their entire executive and management team, or even a majority, are pursuing excellence. An even greater delusion is that unless you have good metrics and accountability structures in place, a large majority of those who rise to leadership positions will be there for the wrong reasons.

YOUR EMPLOYEES

Yes, sometimes your people are the problem. I'm sure you have a great Human Resources department or maybe your organization has "upgraded" the department name to Talent, and it is now run by the Chief Happiness Officer. That alone should have fixed any employee issues you have. Despite your best efforts there is a strong possibility that you have lazy and/or incompetent people in your organization. If you are an executive and this comes as a surprise refer to the section on Executive Team for enlightenment.

As scientifically "proven" in Chapter Two on Synergistic Teams, forming into teams does not take poor employees and make them into star performers. Management training doesn't help either. Before any consideration is given to improving teamwork the right people must be in place. This is sometimes referred to as having the right people "on the bus." Listening to executives and managers claim they

have the right people on the bus to be successful are typically delusional as measured by how successful their bus is.

1. A bus is for customers not employees. If you are setting up a
   bus for the benefit of your employees, it will eventually fail.

2. A bus stops at every block to let people on and off. It will
   pick up anyone that has the fare. Some won't get off when
   they should because they paid the fare and can ride the
   whole route for the same price. Others will exhibit bad
   behavior and will be allowed to stay on the bus.

You don't have time for that. If you must use analogies, I suggest
you trade in the bus for a first-class-only, non-stop train with the following features:

- Your employees are service workers on the train.

- You hire the best workers dedicated to high levels of service.

- You only pick up premium passengers, i.e., profitable
  customers.

- If you do pick up an occasional bad rider you stop and
  let them off.

- If you have non-performing train employees, you do not
  stop. You just throw them off the train.

- Sometimes you need to just unhook a couple of cars with
  both employees and customers and send them off on a side
  track. Bon voyage, et ne reviens pas! This sounds much
  nicer than using the English translation, 'Have a good trip
  and don't come back.'

If you have a team problem you have a people problem, and a people problem can be solved. Unfortunately, it is other people, aka, management people, who must determine what the people problem is. You have now entered the circle of people improvement dysfunctionality and can see why even organizations in a death spiral can't figure out what to do.

PEOPLE IMPROVEMENT CIRCLE OF DYSFUNCTIONALITY

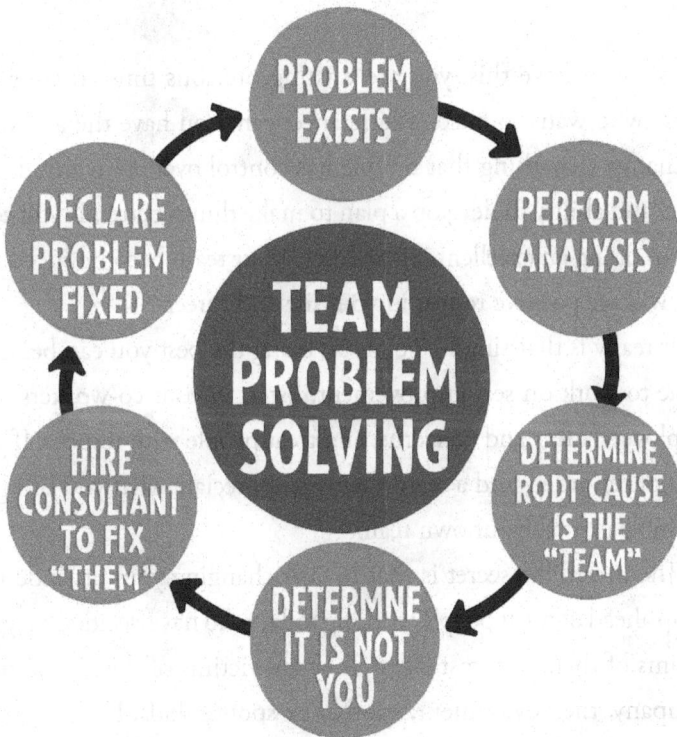

At least you have implemented a standard PowerPoint process cycle that actually comes true when applied.

YOU

Finally, the most important obstacle to your success: You. For those who have been nodding their heads in agreement regarding the preceding analysis on human nature, executives, the boss, and employees there is one other problem you must contend with. Yes, it is you. Here is a statement made by thousands of people around the world every hour.

"I don't have the authority to change anything."

If you believe this, you are wasting precious time in your life. Those who want to make a difference, can. You have the authority to change something that no one has control over: Your mind, attitude, and ability to develop a plan to make things better. If you commit to doing an excellent job and help your team become successful you will see positive results in your life and career.

It really is that simple. Focus on being the best you can be. Continue to work on self-improvement, listen to your co-workers' and employees' ideas and concerns, and treat people with respect. If you are not rewarded find a team that will appreciate what you bring to the table or start your own team.

The incredible secret is that by just changing your attitude you jump ahead of most people working today who have decided they are victims of their circumstances. They are victims of their boss, their company, the government, spouse, ex-spouse, kids, bills, discrimination, climate change, fire ants, alien abductions, or trauma caused by watching the movie "The Last Airbender" after being a fan of the animated series it was allegedly based on. The next step is to just sit on their backsides waiting for a savior to give them what they think they "want." Take the opportunity to earn something for you. All the ills of the world have been here thousands of years. You can sit and whine about it or do something to achieve more in your life. That is your choice regardless of circumstances.

TEAMWORK MOMENT OF TRUTH

No matter how "bad" your manager, employees, or company are behaving, you still have the power to make a difference on your team and in your life.

If you don't believe this "Truth" you are just looking for another silver bullet to "fix" others. You must start with yourself. Only by leading by example will you be able to put the action plans in place outlined in this book and which will make a difference in your organization and individual teams.

OK, after the first three chapters are you depressed? Don't be! Well, OK; depending on your current situation, maybe there is cause for despair. There may be some good news, otherwise known as a glimmer of hope, which may lift you out of your depression. You are officially ahead of many team leaders who have lost sight of the prize and deluded themselves that somehow their executives, managers, and employees are more "special" than thousands of other organizations.

No, it really was your innovative products or services, and some of your team members, which enabled your organization to meet a need in the marketplace at the right time. This is what originally made your organization a success. At the same time, this success was able to cover up weakness in your processes and some of your other team

members. Now that your organization is in trouble or you see problems on the horizon don't expect training programs, software applications, new motivational posters, and executive decrees will fix your
dysfunctional organization and make everyone work together as one
team. Don't follow the lemmings and just make 10% cost reductions
in employees across all areas to be "fair." That just proves you really
are the problem and not a true leader. Now that you admit there is
a problem it is time to make something different happen.

As you begin the exciting journey of building a winning team,
always keep the five obstacles in mind no matter what level of the
organization you find yourself in. Align people with your organizational objectives; provide achievable rewards for success and consequences for failure. If you choose to ignore or delude yourself that
your people are "special" then stop reading. Go ahead and buy that
collaborative work software your Vice President of Visionary Processes recommends to fix your teamwork problem and let me know
how that works out for you.

CHAPTER 4

THE PATH TO TEAM SUCCESS

*"If you don't know where you are going,
any road will get you there."*

LEWIS CARROLL

After reviewing the obstacles in the previous chapters, are you thinking to yourself that all is lost? Perhaps you are. If you are in a state of despair, I don't blame you. The obstacles can be overwhelming, and on some teams may be impossible to remove. It doesn't matter what methodology, management style, or overwhelming evidence of incompetency is demonstrated.

Even if most of the organization understands the problem, sometimes it is beyond hope. If you think you are going to improve the overall operations team when the ICOO, Incompetent Chief Operating Officer, who is married the CEO's brother is leading the team on a death march—good luck! There are teams that must fail spectacularly before anything will change and sometimes what changes is the elimination of the team.

Is there any hope? Indeed, there is hope. Maybe not where you work right now, but hope for you, nevertheless. The hope comes when the leaders of an organization finally decide to cut the "BS," an acronym that stands for Blatant Stupidity, set aside self-delusions about the team, and go to work fixing the problem, including how they are contributing to it. This is a very hard decision that requires a degree of self-awareness and critical examination.

These criteria alone significantly reduce the chances of it happening. Notice that fixing the problem does not include buying software, outsourcing your decisions to consultants, training, or implementing a new methodology or system. This may come as a surprise, but your team problems can't be solved even if you use consultants who claim to be able to leverage AI to make your decisions for you. The only exception to this would be if you use companies that spend a lot of money on social media or televised sporting events about the power of AI solving all the world's problems. Your problems will be easy to fix because these companies are already in the vanguard of ushering in a future AI utopia here on earth. When I hear an executive blo-viate about how they are looking at leveraging AI in their organization my assumption is they haven't started leveraging the first phase of AI, that is, Actual Intelligence. I suggest that should be everyone's first step on their journey of discovery.

Who are the leaders in any organization? The answer is simple yet difficult to execute—those who choose to be. If you don't have the courage and work ethic to make it happen, you will never achieve real success as a leader. That doesn't mean you won't be successful based on your own definition. If your success is defined as having an HR-defined leadership level title, collecting a large salary, empire building, and personal aggrandizement, you can achieve that goal in many organizations without worrying about real organizational team development. If you have committed to being a real team leader there is a path to success. Unfortunately, before we get to that, read on because here comes some more pain to inflict on you first sponsored by organizational reality.

TEAMWORK MOMENT OF TRUTH

There will be no consistent team success without a fundamental understanding and acknowledgment of the individual contribution to that success.

Society has become so immersed in the concept of team performance that the fundamental component of successful teamwork has been lost. That component is the individual. This is in part an outcome from the war on individuality championed by many in government, media, and academia. Individual goal attainment is equated with selfishness and greed while devotion to the betterment of the group is viewed as enlightened thinking and sacrificing one's own needs for the common good. In practice the people who spout this dogma usually mean you need to sacrifice for their common good as opposed to "the" common good. Common good being defined as what the self-appointed judge says common good is. It is also no coincidence that many so called leaders in government, business, and not-for-profit organizations by some miracle manage to turn their words about caring only for the common good into individual good for just them.

From this collectivist logic the belief forms that problems can only be solved by teamwork and large problems solved by even larger teams. Of course, the larger the team the less any individual has accountability for the outcome. Soon there is no one at fault for any problem or lack of solution because the issue is too complex to identify who is responsible. A team, the system, government, management, or external forces, preferably an identified enemy, supernatural being, or other cosmic force must be to blame. When responsibility is removed from individuals by each degree, there is also a corresponding acceptance of any responsibility for outcomes. Success is no longer measured by achievement of goals. It is measured by the good intentions behind the goal even when the problem is not solved or made worse.

Collectivist theory has entered the realm of business practices as well with an emphasis on team objectives and rewards. As in the political world the underlying premise of group reward is usually not recognized as flawed because it is altruistic and good. Individuality is looked upon as potentially harmful to success because it is confused with their definition of selfish behavior. There is also a deeper belief that many humans will not behave correctly unless they are manipulated and/or controlled by those who care about the common good. The first challenge is, who is defining what the common good for any organization and/or team is? This is followed by the challenge of what should be done to achieve this common good. It is natural then to think that having shared common goals and rewards for a team will motivate them to achieve this goal. From this belief leaders have made the leap of faith that putting badly behaved humans on teams will modify their behavior in supporting the achievement of the goal. In fact, it just ruins the entire team.

The more we take away individual creativity and rewards the less output we will receive. Many organizations always look for a "fix" in process or organizational design, thus creating more complexity and bureaucracy no matter how complicated. After all, if a person is at fault, then "blame" might be assigned and feelings hurt. Wrapped into this downward spiral is an almost religious belief that any problem can be solved by a new process as opposed to recognizing that all outcomes and problems can never be anticipated let alone solved. Then you must factor in that regardless of process and systems some people behaving badly will always be a factor, as we discussed in roadblocks to success. Humans are just so darn unpredictable and risky.

The other issue is that even if you solve a problem, you typically create any number of new unanticipated problems and results. Yet every time a major problem occurs, including economic downturns or a business failure, some so-called leader in government and industry claims we can fix this with even more bureaucracy and process, thus ensuring it never happens again. Maybe that exact problem will never happen again, just 500 other problems directly related to your "fix." While it will hurt people's feelings sometimes it is the people, not the process or organizational alignment, that needs to be fixed, and some people can never, ever be "fixed."

TEAMWORK MOMENT OF TRUTH

A great individual performer can overcome a bad business process easier than a great business process can overcome poor individual performers.

Any organization that can return to rational individual rewards will have a competitive advantage. This doesn't mean buying into simplistic Hollywood entertainment concepts of evil businesspeople pursuing profits over people or opposing the glorious workers. It is the acknowledgment that individuals striving to achieve goals produce more benefits to society than attempting to impose group benefits on individuals. Turning workers into drones who must follow more and more rules and regulations, aka process, leads to less creativity and more problems as an output.

The reality is that in today's world most mid-sized to large private entities reflect more of the government team model that is already held up as the savior of individuals. This includes poor managers who are never held accountable for their alleged area of responsibility and an exponential increase in control processes and internal "support" departments that continue to expand their scope. Combine this with lazy and uncommitted people who live off the work of others and you have a recipe for future failure. The only thing that saves a team from failure are individuals who continue to work towards success despite their co-workers and team leaders. The good news is the downward spiral is usually long-term and if you are lucky the customers will continue to buy what you are selling despite whatever model you have implemented.

The utopian team concept of each according to his needs, and if everyone is given a chance they will take advantage of the opportunity, is only true if you have a powerful desire to ignore human history. Many will take advantage of your chance—just not in the way you intend. Once again, a cynical positive outlook comes to the rescue. You should give people an opportunity to succeed knowing there is a chance they will not. It is not a question of being disappointed; just know the probability exists that some people will fail and yes, sometimes it is their fault.

As a team leader you must break out of this trap you have set for yourself with the help of popular culture driven by an attention deficit disorder media and the collectivist utopian dreamers. Team objectives with non-productive individuals create Dysynergy. You can whine about it or wish that humans were not selfish—at least how you define selfish. Then after the whine you can continue to hit people over the head with brute force until they understand how much you care about them. In the end if you don't hold individuals accountable you will get poor team results. If you punish the great individual producers for team results that are caused by the poor performers you gave them, you will fail faster. How do you motivate a team? Maybe it's time to try something different.

TEAMWORK MOMENT OF TRUTH

There will be no team success without individual objectives that are rational and measurable.

It is not enough to have individual objectives. Objectives by themselves in organizations are primarily responsible for hours of mirthless humor by employees as they discuss the latest policy and motivational program developed by the leadership "team." The hard part is how do you determine individual objectives that are rational and measurable? This is followed by the even more difficult action of measuring performance against the objective. First you need to define rational and measurable, otherwise you are leaving the definition open to the possibility of a psychotic "leader" defining both. Of course, none of us have ever seen such a leader at our workplaces, so maybe I shouldn't be worried.

RATIONAL OBJECTIVES

While this may appear to be a statement of the obvious, a rational objective is one you can define; that is appropriate to the person, the job function, and the success of the organization; and that is also achievable. If I tell my marketing manager to design in the next six months a rocket booster that will allow time travel, that would appear to be an irrational metric. In the real-world team individual objectives get close to irrational when not tethered to anything pertaining to reality. Some real-world examples include:

A director told each member of his team that they must improve their production by 40% through productivity improvements. The reason 40% was selected as a metric was because overall team improved their productivity by 20% at the end of last year. The team manager thought that doubling the goal over the next year would provide a "stretch" goal. Why not give them a 1000% objective, what with all the critical thought that was placed in this metric? The first step would be to review how they really achieved the original 20% goal. In reality the process "improvement" was due to a layoff of 20% of the workforce based on seniority in the fourth quarter. The "good" news for the executive that made this decision was his boss didn't see any correlation between this productivity decision and the service contract cancellations that occurred one year later.

In another example, a salesperson had an outstanding year far above any other salesperson in the country, achieving 150% of quota. For the next year the sales manager doubled her individual quota while leaving the quota the same for the rest of the salespeople. When asked why the reasoning was that: "Of course we raised her quota. We paid a significant amount over our "planned" commission sales budget to just her. We need to hit our commission budget next year." If that business logic makes sense to you as a tactic to sustain long-term results, I'm not sure any amount of training is going to help.

These are actual events that "Team Business" has engaged in. Most of you have witnessed or seen much worse, or been a part of these types of objective-setting exercises at some point in your life. The challenge is that one human's psychotic thought processes are another human's idea of rational behavior.

MEASURABLE

Now, sometimes the objective appears rational yet how does one measure it? How about the objective of "90% of our clients believe we bring value." Of course, we want our entire client-facing group to bring value, the challenge is, do you have any ideas on how to measure that? One way to measure it is when a client emails you claiming their account manager Joe is the greatest employee ever in the history of client service. There are a couple of possible reasons this client may have emailed you. Either this proves Joe is bringing value to the client, or Joe has invested a lot of time taking your client to the bar and asking him to email the boss. One client that Joe knows might think you are bringing value (even if Joe's liver might disagree), but does that mean you are bringing a high level of service to all your clients that pay for your service?

Consider the following product strategic objective that is very measurable, which was presented at a strategy session:

Strategy Objective: A key strategy to achieve success is to hire six product analysts.

Hire six product analysts is a team objective? It certainly passes the test of measurability. In fact, it is easily measured and can be surpassed by hiring seven or eight analysts. Is it rational as a strategy objective? At best you can say it is a tactic. Of course, the tactic is really part of the real secret objective:

Secret Strategy Objective: *Build an empire to achieve*
the critical mass necessary to secure the next level
management position.

Everyone knows it, yet for some unfathomable reason no one will put that on the presentation slide. To be charitable the person creating this strategy could also be one of the examples of someone who reached the third level above incompetence and was confusing the number of team members hired with achieving an actual goal. At best you can say it was created by someone not engaging in any critical thought whatsoever. Do you want to guess whether this person received a good rating at the end of the year? You are correct. This team strategy was declared a success.

Sure, you have a metric, and it is measurable. Increase sales by 1000% is a measurable objective as is increase profits by 200%. Is it rational? In most cases it was pulled out of a very dark and bad-smelling place and made an objective because it sounded good for a variety of reasons—usually not related to the business at hand. *Measurable* and *Rational* are intertwined. If only we could apply that to the people developing the objectives. What should these rational and measurable objectives be if not empire building and securing an executive title that you so richly deserve?

TEAMWORK MOMENT OF TRUTH

Every organization can be improved with rational financial and operational metrics that are measurable before building teams.

No $10,000 certification courses, "enterprise" software systems, no purple or mauve belts, and no new made-up languages that only the high priest and her methodology minions know the meaning of. Just give yourself and your organization the FOM treatment—Financial and Operational Metrics. The great thing is that these measurements can be put into place no matter where you are in the organization, including creating your own personal objectives.

Easy to say and perhaps obvious as well, isn't it? If it is obvious then why are there PhDs who are studying why businesses can't consistently execute this simple formula? Thousands of very smart people spend years creating and refining models, tools, and methodologies focused on achieving great results and yet organizations consistently fail to perform. Then one year a miracle happens, and one organization implements the Flight of the Penguins methodology and that very same year becomes successful. The universal business theory has finally been created! Quickly the consultants create programs to help you implement this magic potion of organizational execution. Then two years later the business is failing using the same model.

Yet, why do these models continue to be brought forward? It comes down to a belief that somehow business is a science and that we are one model away from discovering the magic formula that can be applied to every team and individual, thus guaranteeing success. The problem is that using science to support a "belief" tends to promote religious adherence, the creation of worship rituals, and a willingness to cast aside any evidence that doesn't conform to the belief system. This includes an astounding ability to ignore all evidence that your team-building programs don't have any long-term success. The power of synergistic teams is one such cosmic religious token complete with religious artifacts such as the TEAM PLAYER = WINNER coffee mugs.

How could there have been a failure to create the perfect road to team success using motivational speeches and awesome coffee mugs? The challenge is the same as designing logical systems for any dismal science such as economics, business management, sociology, and psychology. Why are they called dismal sciences? While the definition came about in the 19th century in relation to economics, in my view it pertains to any field of study that attempts to take systems that are heavily dependent on human responses and turn them into a scientific repeatable process. Since humans constantly strive for logical answers and take comfort in predictable outcomes it is logical that many fields attempt to predict outcomes based on natural laws or mathematical equations.

In mathematics 2+2 =4; however, in the dismal sciences while we believe it equals 4 there is a subtle and sometimes not so subtle impact of the most unstable element in the universe: the human factor. This human factor creates slight variations to every equation, variations that destroy mathematical models downstream. In analyzing human behavior there is always a slight nuance in the equation. Hidden behind the magic of 2+2 are human variables that impact everything. In the real world instead of equaling four the formula on how a human behaves may be 2+2.05434566 =4.05434566. We may round down to four; however, the outcome expected is no longer "4." When you attempt to apply a formula regarding how different humans will react when faced with the exact same situation the outcome can potentially be wildly different.

All the mathematical formulas contained within complicated system models predicting outcomes are built on assumptions of rational human behavior. Scientific projection models are unstable enough when you are trying to predict natural events such as weather with thousands of climate systems and variables in action. If you try to calculate irrational human behavior into your model, including probability and impact, you are on the border of just becoming the local carnival mystic predicting the future for money. For a good example refer to your stock analyst predicting what stock prices will do next week. It is typically even worse since models are built using the assumptions of what rational human behavior should be in the eyes of another "so-called" rational human. Good luck turning human behavior controlled by a series of chemical impulses that are unique in every brain into scientific process that determines how people will consistently behave. A quick review of reality television shows and social media posts should eliminate any doubt you have of predicting rational human behavior.

Now it is time to attempt to solve your teamwork problems and remember this Teamwork Moment of Truth.

TEAMWORK MOMENT OF TRUTH

Business is an art and so is teamwork.

Yes, business is not a science no matter how much the business professor wants to be considered in the upper echelon of academia much like those arrogant mathematicians. The underlying principles are not complicated. The dilemma is that the application of the art of management can be extremely difficult depending on the canvas where you work and the results you are attempting to achieve. Even if everything is the same, including the humans running the system, over time human responses will change, creating a breakdown in the overall process. The perfect system that delivers the financial and quality results you are looking for one year can later become your demise as any number of inputs to the perfect system change, creating a formula that no longer functions as planned.

Once you realize that it is an art that needs to constantly be evaluated and altered based on a thousand variables you can set free those dreams of finding a systematic solution that will solve all your team problems forever. You can then begin the journey to find real solutions to real problems with your broken processes and people while understanding that next year it might not work.

This is one of many reasons the so-called popular methodologies and trends holding up a particular CEO or company become a business case on what not to do just a few years later. We see something that works and immediately attempt to research and produce repeatable processes to replicate the results in other areas. If you peel back these allegedly "new" reasons for success you see the exact same reasons dressed up in new languages and repackaged methodologies. It is also why you get completely different results.

This is what happens when you spend too much time in the microanalysis of human behavior. It becomes unhelpful and you start to forget what problem exactly we were attempting to solve before we, meaning you, descended into organizational behavior and psychology to figure out how to make those wacky team members productive.

THE FUNDAMENTAL
BUILDING BLOCKS OF SUCCESS

It's time to stop looking for that magical force that will solve all your problems. No matter what you think the problem is on your team, before doing anything it's time to go back to the basics. For an overall organizational team and the teams contained within to be successful you must have the two critical components firmly defined: Financial and Operational Objectives.

They are THE only two areas of importance that you must get serious about first. Both must be created and balanced to have long-term success. After these are in place for the overall team both must then be created for every individual contributor from the CEO right down to every individual team member in order for you to achieve the success you are looking for—or at least the success you say you are looking for. Both must be in place before you can even begin to consider the question of whether you have the right people to achieve your team goals? How can you really know if you have "the right people on the train" as we discussed previously if you don't have the right team objectives in place?

After, and only after, the first two building blocks are in place, do you proceed with the third building block—people. Yes, the people on the team should be the last thing you look at. Until you do you have no idea if your people are actually your most important asset to success. This includes all the leaders who drone on about how their people are their most important asset. The leaders who constantly say that are usually the ones who don't have a clue who reporting to them might qualify as an important asset.

TEAMWORK MOMENT OF TRUTH

If you can't articulate how any "people" you hire directly impact your financial and operational objectives, you have no idea whether they are team assets or a pain in the "missing ETS."

TRANSLATING TEAM OBJECTIVES
INTO INDIVIDUAL OBJECTIVES

The path to success is for leaders to first recognize why their company, department, and own personal employment exists. Confront the real obstacles that must be faced for the business to succeed. Then put concrete measurements in place for yourself, your department, and your company. While most leaders will claim they already do this, in reality they put window curtains up to hide serious problems with the inside structure. Complicated models and methodologies are mixed with slogans that achieve nothing.

If individual financial and operational objectives can fix any team, where do you start? While we all may agree that rational financial and operational objectives should be a part of every individual's performance, there is a major obstacle to overcome. Assigning individual objectives and measures is hard work and will result in a certain amount of conflict. Conflict has been demonized as a bad thing in the media, books, and classroom. When you think conflict you think the Middle East conflict, wars, or maybe a bad personal relationship. There are many people who believe they would rather have a conflict-free existence even though in practice this is an impossible human state. You can delay the inevitable and always give in, which causes frustration and lack of performance over the long term. Unfortunately, you can't remove conflict from the human equation.

Of course, the other way to avoid team conflict is to just create fuzzy team goals that are always open to interpretation. Then send out emails or pronouncements on occasion exhorting the team to do better. This has the advantage of allowing the team leader to change the goals and objectives at any time. Even better, distribute motivational team posters such as this around your organization:

为加速实现农业机械化而奋斗

chineseposters.net

Nothing motivates people like a poster that exhorts the workers to "Struggle to speed up the realization of agricultural mechanization." If you decide that won't work, then it may be that actual financial and operational objectives are the magic elixir that can be applied to your team.

What do you find when you peek behind the current overall team balance sheet that provides the obvious performance data on these two critical items? Typically, fuzzy financial and operational objectives that vary depending on positions and functions and with unclear performance metrics. Determining traditional metrics, measuring, and insisting on performance to standards is hard work and will result in conflict with non-performers. Your boss certainly isn't demanding it, and you wanted to be a team manager for prestige and more money. The only work you want to do is create the presentation slides that say, "We are unleashing our synergistic work teams through collaborative relationship software to enable us to capture increased market share." If you are not one of "them" it's time to take a journey through each building block of team success in the next chapters.

CHAPTER 5

BUILDING BLOCK #1: FINANCIAL OBJECTIVES

"It is better to have a permanent income than to be fascinating."

OSCAR WILDE

I f you are committed to follow the path to team success, it's time to explore each area in more detail starting with financial objectives. There are many theories, books, and team leader discussions regarding how to provide financial incentives to individuals who work on a team. The problem is that before you can assign individual financial objectives that will provide long-term incentives you must first have rational financial objectives for the overall team. In other words, why do you even have a team to begin with? Let's again state the obvious. Every organization must measure financials—that is, the cost, revenue, and profit that support the goals and strategies of the organization. I didn't say they had to measure it well, as demonstrated every year by organizations that go bankrupt or team executives who receive felony convictions for their accounting fables. At the very top of the team organization this is clear or should be. Before you attempt to create individual financial objectives the first step is to determine if the overall financial objectives of the team are legitimate. What are you truly measuring?

> ## TEAMWORK MOMENT OF TRUTH
>
> Creating individual financial objectives is useless or destructive unless built upon solid overall financial objectives.

Well, wasn't that moment of truth obvious? The problems start when those humans we discussed previously get to define "solid overall financial objectives." Revenue must exceed expenses and make a profit for the overall team at some point. Perhaps a clarification is in order; real revenue should exceed real expenses and make a real profit at some point. It's the definition of "real" and "at some point" that get people into "real" trouble at "some point." It is also a fact that at some point our sun will die billions of years from now. This is about the same time some of your products or acquisitions will make money for the team.

Most organizations will claim their financial metrics are very good and can prove it with hundreds of complex spreadsheets and reports. Of course, that's what you say. What are you going to tell stockholders and the board of directors? That you are always surprised every quarter when the overall financial reports are run? No matter what financial analysis system you use, accounting methodology, and budgeting practices, at the end of the day the owners want to know if the team made money or need to reconsider their investment choice. There are quite a few organizations that can answer yes to making money for one quarter or a year or two. The question is, was it real money or "creative accounting money," followed by, how sustainable are those positive financials, and do you care?

This brings up the most difficult yet the most important indicator of whether you have a truly well-run organizational team financially. Well-run companies achieve sustainable REAL positive financial results over a five-year horizon. Unfortunately, we confuse real results with pretending to achieve real results. There are three general ways to pretend to achieve real results:

- Slash—Burn—Exterminate.
- Float down the River Denial.
- Create Exciting Infomercials.

SLASH—BURN—EXTERMINATE

Anyone, including a Chief Financial Officer with a master's degree in finance, can make a team profitable for one or two years. For example, just lay off 20% of the work force without regard to contribution, sell your office buildings, and outsource large areas of operations. Then you can claim massive productivity gains and reap the financial rewards for your company. Of course, it is a nice surprise when you realize your smart decisions also increased your personal executive team bonus that year. This is by far the most used methodology and will enable most teams, no matter how mismanaged, to reach a short-term financial objective. The downside is that in most cases the people making the decisions are the principal obstacles to success we discussed previously and who got the team into this mess to begin with. Since the real issues with the team were never addressed the downward spiral begins, creating round after round of "rightsizing."

This sounds much better than fired or exterminated—at least to the ones who were not part of the "rightsizing."

Since the executives don't have a clue regarding where the problem is and there are no mirrors available for self-reflection, arbitrary target numbers are assigned to each area regardless of performance. This creates the idiotic result of one team full of 500 boat anchors only losing ten percent of their team in a "rightsize" initiative instead of the ninety percent that would go if anyone was measuring anything important to the overall company team objectives. At the same time the team that performed well, bringing value to the overall team and making up for the useless team's failure, also must "rightsize" by ten percent. Is it any wonder that most teams that embark on this course do not have a happy ending unless by some miracle the company is acquired, or one product comes along and saves them—at least temporarily—at the last minute.

FLOAT DOWN THE RIVER DENIAL

On the other end of the spectrum are the teams that spend most of their time manipulating numbers on spreadsheets. This is a time-honored tradition to create the illusion that everything is going just great. There are hundreds of accounting tricks available that enable you to push out costs to some future date while you wish and hope for a miracle. Like that product that needs just a few more years of losing money before it produces one billion dollars after you achieve "market momentum." Reality eventually catches up and you become a Harvard business case that students can say, oh yes isn't it obvious why they failed? Ever notice how few of these geniuses are around with their "obvious" analysis before a team fails?

You can also pretend to make money through alleged productivity improvements. This enables you to believe you are doing something to achieve real financial objectives. For example, your Information Technology team may be burning millions of dollars on "cutting-edge" software that appears to get the big team zero return in actual productivity or revenue yet adds huge real operational cost. If someone starts to question the cost, you see more smoke bombs and theatrics than an old rock band concert reunion tour. When the show is over you say, wow, that was a great show. Does anyone remember what was played? No, but we do know what to do about it. Bury it in operational overhead, reallocate the costs, or move it into a different cost center and then let the justifications begin. To save you some time here are some bullet points you can give marketing so they can start creating the appropriate "message."

- We are investing in infrastructure to contribute long-term productivity enabling sustainable growth.

- We are beginning the journey to transform into an AI technology-driven company to compete in an evolving dynamic marketplace.

- We are pivoting to enable the ability to capture additional market share through strategic investments and acquisitions.

When all else fails claim you built the infrastructure to enable product development or sales, and due to unforeseen market conditions have reduced earnings expectations. If you are floating down the River Denial, feel free to use any of these. While they are old excuses the classics never go out of style.

Product development is another great way to hop on the all-expense paid river denial boat tour. I have seen many presentations where the team reports that everything is going well and we are on target. The problem is the "target" apparently moves based on the alignment of the planets. There are twenty presentation slides with awesome graphics showing the great momentum that is being achieved. If forced to provide it there may be one slide that shows the horrendous financial numbers that are glossed over. No worries, just quickly move to the next slide stating that while sales and profits are down right now due to many unforeseen events, the team is poised for incredible growth next year. The great thing is if the numbers don't work one year blame current economic conditions, exchange rates, sunspots, headwinds, asteroid collisions, alien invasions, and general unforeseen circumstances. You can then recycle the same presentation slides for next year's "targets," saving time and thereby increasing productivity "savings" in your area. Win-Win!

Once you start playing financial games on the river of denial then budgeting games and rationalization for poor performance become the focal point of everyone including the CEO, taking away from the true focal point of why your team was in business to begin with. If you are a CEO, or part of the executive team, don't blame your individual circus performers—at least not all of them. You created this circus and provided the incentives to keep the big tent full of fake activity. When executives and managers are awarded based on achieving their "budget," the amount of praise they are giving their boss regarding their dynamic leadership, or the size and graphic content of their presentations, you get exactly that.

TEAM INFOMERCIAL FINANCIALS

Then there is the third way to look successful. Create a team that appears to have a product or vapor concept that creates buzz in the marketplace and possibly even attracts more investment money. If the trick works the stock price explodes, incredible market capitalization is achieved, and it appears the team is positioned to dominate the market. Business "thought leaders" and media outlets deduce that there is one key reason that explains this development. The team is run by leaders who have cast away old business models and developed a new path to success. Consultants then pile on claiming it is time to embrace the new paradigm. Game rooms, open spaces, dedication to social responsibility, winner of the greatest place in the universe to work, attention to the needs of Generation "fill in the blank," and other nonsensical reasons are given for success of this team.

The problem is when the bottom falls out after a couple of years, or longer based on how much funding is rolling in, all that is left is a grossly inefficient cost model that collapses at the first sign of trouble. It was a giant Ponzi scheme with the media supplying glowing accounts for the new business model while the team leaders were betting on finding some sucker to buy them before the crash. Sometimes it works. Sometimes it doesn't.

Even if you can't generate a "Team Wow" infomercial effect in the public arena, no worries. Generate the same effect internally to ensure a continued cash flow for your personal team, i.e., bank account. Create an "out-of-the-box" idea to make millions to pitch to the board or executives; watch them get excited. You can then appeal to their need for something new and shiny to talk about and/ or their desire to make a lot of money. Generate buzz with internal promotional items, presentations to the board, seminars, web pages, internal announcements, etc.

Even if you lose millions of dollars for the team you have ensured a salary for at least a couple of years before even the dumbest team

CEO figures out this isn't working. There are cases where not even the most clueless CEO or Board of Directors figures it out. Just remember to always speak passionately about the future of the team financials. We are moving to the promised land! Don't ever underestimate the power of team wow infomercials mixed with heavy self-promotion.

For the most creative team leaders, various tactics within each of these strategies can be combined to create a unique plan customized to fool everyone for as long as possible. If you have decided not to use one of the three typical team financial strategies and are committed to using real financial metrics to measure team success, there remains a difficult obstacle. No matter what financial strategy you use when it comes to financial accountability after the overall balance sheet at the next level on the team the financials immediately start to blur. The further down in an organizational structure you go, and the larger the organization becomes, the more disconnected people are from the main point, the raison d'être, for having their job on the team in the first place. Hey, what was the reason this company or organization was created to begin with? This brings up another Teamwork Moment of Truth.

TEAMWORK MOMENT OF TRUTH

A team making their financial plan is not the same as being successful.

Several Chief Financial Officers just put my face on a dart board. If your reason for being in business is to just make a pile of money in one year, why are you even reading a book on teamwork and improving performance? Whack all the support staff, create an impressive web site that says our customers are our top priority, and quickly sell off before anyone figures it out. Do you really need a consultant to figure that out other than to provide you with political cover because you have no courage, are incompetent, or both? Either way you should quickly call a recruiter to start looking for another team based on your current "success". Once again you can blame lack of execution by others for the failure after you leave.

If you are interested in running a long-term organization, you must ensure you build real financial objectives before any attempt at setting real individual rewards. The definition of real financials is not what you wish for. Real Financials are what is possible in your industry balanced with the other building blocks that we will discuss in the next chapters. Making the quarterly "plan" targets is not the same as long-term financial viability. If you don't change to realistic team objectives, real individual financial accountability towards long-term objectives is impossible. You are just creating a lot of complicated spreadsheets, adjustments, and smoke and mirrors every year. This translates into creating stupid financial compensation plans to allegedly motivate your team members.

You have a solid overall financial plan. Are you sure? Really sure? OK, we'll take your word for, so now is the time for the real work to begin. Every position and every person on the team must be justified by how they contribute to the success of the team, including revenue and profitability. Every manager must have accountability for the profitability of the overall team instead of managing "their" budget. What does financial accountability mean? Who exactly is financially accountable for what? Accountability means everyone needs to feel the pain and rewards of financial accountability for their area of influence because that is why your team exists

TEAMWORK MOMENT OF TRUTH

If there is not any monetary value to the team associated with the work, it is not worth doing.

Now some CFOs are taking my picture off the dart board, at least for a minute. The preceding Moment of Truth is a major sin against the latest religion of virtue signaling and dragging your organization into controversial social and political issues because people with an agenda are demanding it. Your business or organization was created to bring value for the owners and your customers, not responding to the demands of social media mobs, or worse your desire to signal you own virtue or advance your personal agenda as you claim to speak for the team. When you drift from the mission of your team you will create fewer jobs, endanger the long-term viability of your company, and in the end provide FEWER benefits to society. I have one caveat to this statement. If you are beholden to the government for your revenue, or your industry is heavily regulated, you must also pay homage to what your government masters say is important to a greater extent. Never attempt to fool yourself that this is anything but an additional cost of doing business.

This also applies to leaders who demand their employees participate in their favorite charities, or worse, pressure employees to contribute money to their favorite charity with payroll deductions. You can claim it is voluntary all you want but most of your team members will feel compelled to comply. After all, who wants to look like they don't support a great charity that the boss loves? Forced charity is not the definition of charity. If you are a leader who does this, chances are very high you are too obtuse and egocentric to understand the ramifications of your virtue signaling to your team.

Beware of team leaders swaddling themselves in virtue while claiming it is not about the money in their organization. When reading or hearing this my eyes involuntarily roll so far back that there is a distinct chance they will be stuck permanently against my cranium. The challenge to that statement is that at the end of the day it is about the money if you want to continue as a long-term successful entity. This includes charitable organizations and other "not-for-profit" entities. You will not be successful if your entire team is not aware of the importance of meeting realistic financial goals and their role in doing so. If you can't identify how a particular team contributes to the financial success of the overall team, then the organization should be eliminated.

Now is not the time to rationalize how a particular team is "contributing." The Office of Visionary Product Processes needs to be removed from your operating expenses. The Senior Vice President for strategic projects, who has no strategic projects, should be asked to pursue other interests. Admit you created a job out of thin air for someone you like. Long-term friendships, dressing well, drinking with the boss, or enjoying time at the golf course are not to be confused with bringing value to a team. If you are weak and can't let "non-value add" employees go, simply send them home with a check and promise you will keep them away from the rest of the team producers. At least your other team members won't have to put up with seeing them act like they have an important job. This helps eliminate

Dysynergy as well. An additional benefit will be fewer meetings scheduled to bother people with the latest posters they are creating for the hallway. Categorize this on the balance sheet as WEUOPEX (Weak Executive Unnecessary Operating Expense).

Identifying financial accountability for each position does not translate into every position tied to direct sales at some type of retail level. That will create a different type of operational havoc and misplaced priorities. What it does mean is every job on the team must be reviewed to determine how the position contributes to the financial results of the team. In turn, everyone must understand how they support the viability of the overall team either directly or indirectly. This also supports setting up reward structures that encourage helping other teams when needed to improve the financial performance of the overall team. If you really want cost savings and process improvement, then create an environment where every team member understands how every dollar of real cost they remove from the equation doesn't just help the "team." It also helps the individual team member in some way

This awareness must be more than a general understanding of the team's finances. Every person must be able to tell you how they contribute and how they MEASURE their contribution. Don't want to tell your employees financial information and how they contribute? Why? What are you hiding? Do you not have any measurements in place to tell them? If you have the data, do you not trust what you claim is your most important asset—your people? If there is no trust maybe you don't have the "best" people in the industry. Maybe you don't want to tell them they are funding the "No profitability for the next 10 years" department down the hall because you think it would be bad for morale. Guess what? They already know they are funding your bad decisions.

WHO DETERMINES
FINANCIAL ACCOUNTABILITY?

Now it's time for the CFOs to once again put my face back up on the dart board. Establishing financial goals and direction of the company should not be the Chief Financial Officer's role. Why not? After all, it's right there in the title, Chief Financial Officer. There are several challenges with this. An accounting and finance background generally translates into looking at a business vision as maximizing revenue and margin. This is sometimes dressed up as strategic finance thinking, but it really is just basic accountant thinking. While financial accountability and performance must be key pillars, what are the right financial metrics to have for the overall organization? What are the short, as well as the long-term goals, for the organization that translate into financial targets and investment decisions? What are the realistic margin goals based on the industry and the products the company has created now and into the future?

CFOs are typically not wired to balance these decisions well in determining the Financial Goals. This doesn't mean they are not pivotal in these discussions. Someone needs to ask the hard financial questions when determining the goals of the organization and providing a counterbalance for the wildly idiotic things other executives may be proposing to explain the financial impact. Of course, I am assuming your CFO is special. Nevertheless, if a CEO outsources their leadership role to the CFO out of incompetence, laziness, or both; your goals will typically become unbalanced toward short-term financial targets. That could be the precursor to long-term failure. If you want to make matters worse allow the CFO to expand their role into other areas of operations. As discussed in Chapter 2, CFOs who make it to this executive team position are not immune from what happens to other executive positions. There is a tendency to focus on expanding their importance as well as the scope and size of their organization. In these situations, they are no longer neutral arbiters of the company finances and the budgeting process for the CEO. They are now in the game.

Before addressing financial accountability, the entire executive team needs to be on the same page with the CEO in taking responsibility for realistic financial goals. Without this buy-in you can't drive the correct financial accountability goals to all areas of the organization and also create operational success.

ADDRESSING FINANCIAL ACCOUNTABILITY

Most team leaders will say in fact they do address financial accountability. Exhibit A in demonstrating this is called the department cost center model. As teams become larger the problem with managing to cost centers generates a real potential of separating various sub-teams from the whole point of the overall goals. It also has the effect of focusing management energy on validating why they must have a certain budget number in each individual line item.

After a while a team manager is judged on how well each general accounting ledger item is doing against "plan" as opposed to managing a portion of the business to achieve the overall team objectives. In theory, of course, this should help keep operating costs down, as each division, supposedly responsible for allocating funds based on what is needed for success, strives to stay "on budget". Great theory—bad reality. There are three reasons this creates a bad reality:

1. Anyone can rationalize how their cost center will help the overall team, even if it is ten years into the future.

2. It spurs adversarial relationships between cost centers as they try to grab as much of the "free" budget money as possible.

3. The goal becomes spending the money because a budget variance shows you are not a good financial manager. It then becomes the "perfect" socialist government model where no one is even talking about what the business is about. It's all about feeding the Ministry of Truth the right agricultural numbers.

Taken to the extreme, to control costs, you can get managers managing to general ledger line items, so they create control processes like three levels of approval to order a box of pencils. The good news is you were able to justify spending an excessive amount of money on a supply chain ordering system, enabling you to add three levels of approvals for ordering the pencils while tracking each subaccount down to the penny. The bad news is the system is hard to use, requires upgrades and maintenance and three developers to support. Of course, that is over in General Ledger Cost Department 666, therefore it is not your problem how that boondoggle was funded.

By definition, managers are tactical. If you reward based on managing to cost centers, you will get management to cost centers. Operational efficiency and meeting budgetary targets should tie directly to the tactical performance of not just their team, but the division and company as well. Financial targets should then be tied to their monetary compensation. Want to see if financials are aligned in your organization? How many cost center teams look to give their money and head count to other areas without being asked to help the overall business or solve some other team's budget problem? Hey, where did everyone go?

INCENTIVE PROGRAMS

On some level either consciously or unconsciously many team executives have recognized that financial accountability and motivation
of individuals to achieve financial goals of the organization is a good
thing. The team leader might have even read a book on the topic.
They also might have figured out that cost center management isn't
that great of a tool for teams or individual financial accountability.
There may even be a recognition that performance appraisals and
budgeting don't provide the motivation needed to achieve team goals.
The next response is usually that a team has indeed already incorporated individual incentives to create financial accountability into their
compensation plan. Yes, we do reward top performers; it's called the
annual bonus program.

There have been thousands of studies on how to create great bonus
programs and some even contain examples of programs that worked,
at least in the beginning. Now maybe by some miracle your team
created one of these great bonus programs that started out rewarding individuals appropriately. The odds are not in your favor; however, for the purpose of discussion we will make that assumption.
Programs that start out with the best intentions, and appear to provide incentives to team members, typically devolve into some very
bad behaviors that have nothing to do with accountability or motivation towards team success.

TEAMWORK MOMENT OF TRUTH

Every team member loves an overall company performance bonus unless you don't give it to them.

The first problem is that after a few years a global organizational bonus based on some metric detached from an employee's day-to-day function becomes expected. Everyone is working hard in my department therefore we all deserve a bonus. The question is working hard doing what? Generating more cost? It also encourages some of those pesky humans on the team to "game" the system, including the executives who are also compensated based on the goals outlined in the bonus program. A bonus based on the financial results of the team sounds good on paper. The problem as we discussed earlier is the further you get from the CEO level the more disconnected the overall team results are from the daily work a team member does.

While you may have a bonus program it is not effective unless you have three components:

1. Is your bonus program tied directly to financial performance?

2. Do your employees see a direct correlation between the work they do and their bonus?

3. Are there other operational components included that must be met besides just overall financial performance?

Without these components a bonus program is more likely a demotivator for people working to achieve team goals when it is disconnected from what they do, and they have no influence over results. This happens when a CEO or executive team confuses their accountability with people "lower" on the team food chain. It is also one of the few times most executives start to really believe in pure socialism. Hey, the "team" didn't make the numbers which means everyone will only receive 70% of the bonus. Congratulations, you saved money, hid the reason behind not making the overall numbers this year, and have just killed productivity for the next two years as people who met all their agreed-to objectives are punished. For the people responsible for the financial decline, including the executives in charge, they are given a bonus for failing and encouragement to continue along the same path.

This is viewed as a normal and logical executive response to not making the numbers, yet it isn't applied to all areas. If your team has a sales department with ten salespeople and two bring in 10 million dollars and four bring in zero, do you take the commission away from the two salespeople who were successful because the others didn't make their numbers? Doubtful if anyone thinks that is a good idea. If you do, I suspect there may be a leadership position waiting for you in the People's Republic of Utopia where salespeople are paid each according to your perception of their needs. Back in the real world the top salesperson makes their "bonus" regardless of how the overall company did. Why? There is a direct relationship between the person's individual sales objective and their salary, i.e., commission bonus.

The key is that when one looks at commission-based sales the answer is obvious. Yet somehow if a division vice president is running their business into the ground why do companies make their team members suffer in a totally different subsidiary by lowering their bonus? The easy answer is we had to because Mr. VP of Crazy Ideas gave a Team Wow Infomercial to his CEO and just sucked 10 million out of the budget that everyone else must make up. If you are currently in this camp, consider how this creates a situation where no one believes their extra effort is in any way tied to the performance of the overall team. In turn this creates an environment where extra effort is not forthcoming. The team members just hope the financials turn out this year. If you decide to push the financial objectives for bonus further and further down, you must make the financial rewards real for the people involved. There is a very good reason why this isn't done by team leaders. It is difficult, time-consuming, and the people making the bonus decisions may be part of the roadblocks to success, such as by causing the wrong behaviors to be rewarded.

SHOULD FINANCIAL OBJECTIVES BE CREATED OUTSIDE OF SALES?

One of the objections about providing financial objectives and accountability to people not in sales is that good people who are not money motivated will leave. Obviously, money is not the only motivator for most people and when it is the only metric it creates bad behavior and some long-term team sustainability problems. The point is that if your team was created to make a profit, I am suggesting you think about having people work for you who care about such matters. If you counter that people also demand a great work environment in addition to money, I concur to a certain extent. Unfortunately, there has been too much attention focused on this latest fad for several reasons, including human resource departments attempting to expand their importance within an organization, and a general delusion that it is important because "experts" say it is important. A cynical optimist may also think there is a very small probability that it is promoted because it is cheaper than paying team members more money while showing how much team leadership cares.

Another objection is that some team members don't like being held accountable for financial performance and it will be a demotivator. What most people object to is accountability for things that are not within their control to influence. Your job is to throw out that archaic system you have now and make it tangible to every employee no matter what they do. If they still don't like being held accountable, then give them to the competition. The real reason this isn't done is because the executive team can't pinpoint the areas within each division responsible for an appropriate financial objective. Even if by some miracle the leadership team can assign a financial component to each area the task of assigning the appropriate monetary value for achieving a bonus, even if the overall organization fails to achieve its numbers, is a bridge most leaders will not cross.

If you are going to have an incentive bonus for your individual contributors, it should be structured to ensure that every person on the factory floor or service representative exceeding their numbers receives the bonus if deserved. This should be the case even if the company did not perform overall as well as it should have except in the most extreme circumstances. You also need to ensure your incentives include financial rewards around assisting other individual and teams to support the overall team goals. It is not helpful to punish a person who didn't make their "financial plan" because they were asked to help another team on the edge of disaster, a disaster that would have resulted in a significant impact to the success of the overall organization's goals.

If the organization doesn't achieve its goals the first people who don't get their bonus should be the CEO and the executive committee. That rarely happens because the team leaders have already determined they created an absolutely brilliant plan and the only reason for failure was poor execution by the team below them. Conversely, if the company didn't perform well yet everyone is making their bonus, this indicates your incentive plan may not be measuring the right metrics. If you don't cross this personal financial accountability bridge then Ms. or Mr. Team CEO you are punishing high-performing teams for the errors and lack of success by others and putting yourself in a downward spiral.

WHAT SHOULD YOU DO FROM A BUDGETING PERSPECTIVE?

First, stop what you are doing. Ask the hard questions now before the next year's budgeting process begins. What does every team do to support bringing revenue and profit into the organization? Some will have less than they should, and some will have more. I have not seen any organization that could not have at least a ten percent redeployment of positions internally to more productive efforts. Of course, the ten percent number doesn't apply to your team since you have honed your metrics to perfection. The only logical conclusion is you need to add 50 more people to the budget request. We are just talking about the "other" teams. Second, review your bonus program to be sure it isn't an entitlement and truly is a "bonus." Then work to make it meaningful. People get disillusioned funding your bad business decisions through their personal bonus. That is exactly the message you send when you lower bonuses based on the performance of other areas.

If you can't explain the role of each position in your organization and how it contributes financially to success, that is a sign of trouble. One of the worst ways to assign a bonus number at the individual level is to have each employee create their personal goals. There are several reasons team leaders think this is a great idea:

1. Gives the illusion that an employee is setting their goals and will work hard to make them as opposed to working

hard to create individual stretch goals, such as, "I promise to show up to work 80% of the time."

2. Gives HR more power in an organization since they are typically in charge of the goal-setting process. As an added benefit they can now belly up to the capital request feeding trough for that expensive employee engagement goal-setting software and report on how many people have completed the goal tasks.

3. Setting goals for each individual is hard work and who wants to do that? Better to just type in some generic goals and hit send. At the end of the day the boss will give you the rating they want. As a bonus HR can "empower" all team members to figure out and submit their own individual goals in a centralized cloud-based AI-supported HR application. This demonstrates that HR also supports the company automation efforts while leveraging the latest tech.

If you can't figure out how to create an individual bonus program that truly reflects what the individual does to support the team you are better off not having a structured bonus program at all. Create a simple across-the-board, percentage-based bonus based only on company financial performance that year if you like having a bonus program. Don't worry, the people on your team will still complain about the bonus program. The good news is it will be much less expensive to manage and just as motivational as the convoluted one you have in place now.

In summary, you must have financial objectives that directly relate to what the team members work on to achieve the team, i.e., organizational, goal of success and then reward them financially for this success. You can't have individual objectives unless your overall objectives for the team are real. Every reward has a financial component. Even if you reward them with another day off, show them the financial aspect of that decision. It is not "free" so don't act like it is by saying nonsense like I can't give you a raise, but I can give you another day off. If you use an incentive bonus program, make sure it is incenting something you care about. Otherwise, it will become another source of Dysynergy when your team realizes that it is arbitrary and not tied to any contribution they make.

The worst thing you can do is create a bonus incentive program and then give out bonuses based on how the CEO or executives "feel" about how a division, team, or individual contributed. Now that you have the financials in place you can't stop. You have two more legs to put on the stool of teamwork or else all your hard work in the financials area will be a monumental waste of time in the pursuit of long-term success for your team. Time to move to the next chapter and discover some more "secrets" on how to run a successful team.

CHAPTER 6

BUILDING BLOCK #2: OPERATIONAL OBJECTIVES

*"No enterprise can exist for itself alone. It ministers
to some great need, it performs some great service,
not for itself, but for others; or failing therein, it
ceases to be profitable and ceases to exist."*

CALVIN COOLIDGE

Everyone has heard the famous saying that the only thing matters is the bottom line. One can assume they mean financial results, even if in reality they confuse the bottom line with driving the team to hit rock bottom with every action they take. While extremely important and in some cases forgotten about, the real "bottom line" is not just financial performance. If it was your boss would give you a gun and say go rob people on the corner every day. OK, maybe your boss does tell you to do that; however, in general most businesses want to make money and continue to make money. This means you must balance your financial objectives with operational objectives to sustain a long-term business venture. This may be a difficult concept for some members of the finance team to understand. Unfortunately, at point you must produce something of value that works as intended to keep creating those new accounting methods, and innovative ways to count beans.

Every organization must have financial and operational metrics. If you have poor operational metrics, you will get what you ask for, including pressure on quarterly results sacrificing the long-term health of the overall team and possibly unethical financial reporting methodologies by your direct reports. After all you are only about quarterly financials, right? If the preceding statement is true, my prediction is at minimum you will be asked to leave at some point. On the other end of the scale there is a potential congressional hearing or court appearance in your future.

I have good news for those of you planning to disappear to a country that has "elected" a president for life and welcomes contributions that allow you to live off your ill-gotten gains. Nothing we are talking about should be a roadblock to continuing down your current path. Another option that may provide a more legal way to run a scam is to build a Team Wow company. The goal would then be to get acquired quickly before anyone figures out your creative accounting methodologies while talking about a future nirvana of unlimited easy money.

If those two options are not part of your business plan, operational metrics are needed to balance the financial metrics in all aspects. If you have a customer retention goal of ninety percent and a goal of increasing new sales by ten percent you must have the appropriate products, staff, and tools to achieve those objectives. Therefore, you accept the financial cost of those decisions as part of your business model. If you don't have great operational metrics and just overpromise and under deliver, your team's position in the marketplace will suffer at some point and impact those financial metrics you claim to care about.

Do people need a business degree to figure this out? The answer of course is no. Unfortunately, like every other concept in this book you might already understand what you need to do operationally and/ or recognize the importance intuitively. The challenge is you have a difficult time stepping back from the pressures of each day's management crisis to be able to change the dynamics on your team. I am giving you the benefit of the doubt here since it is also entirely possible that some team leaders have never understood any these concepts, or care at all about the team unless it impacts their personal financial situation. Either way you have my permission to use this excuse for not performing the appropriate management functions for your team up to this point.

It is easy to lose sight of the obvious things that make teams successful. Yes, there are other businesses that appear to succeed without using these principles. Organizations that rely on financial tricks and quarterly business plans to impress investors typically produce nothing of long-term value and are unsustainable. Monopolies, and to a certain extent oligopolies, are example of enterprises that don't necessarily have to follow proven management principles short term. In the end events usually catch up with every endeavor, including those that believe they will never have to compete. What do operational objectives have to do with teamwork?

TEAMWORK MOMENT OF TRUTH

There can be no teamwork without appropriate and understood operational goals and metrics around what each individual must do to achieve the team goal.

OK, but what is an acceptable operational goal? Customer satisfaction is a global answer that is the holy grail of service. The challenge is the measurement as it pertains to each team is more difficult to ascertain. Of course, you must have some sort of customer satisfaction with your product or service even if you are the State Department of Motor Vehicles. The question is where you fall in the customer satisfaction continuum, followed by asking yourself where you should be.

Customer Satisfaction Continuum

The Customer Satisfaction Continuum is important for two reasons.

Reason 1: If you achieve what your customers hope for there is the potential of a long-term loyal customer.

If you achieve what they barely tolerate you have created an opening for the competition.

The team leader is the one who needs to step up and define the operational goals. Why do you have to define it? A team where everyone has different definitions of quality, service, performance, and delivery is a team heading for failure on every level. You also must determine where you really want to be on the continuum as opposed to the self-delusion that you want to be #1 in customer service. No, you don't, or we, your customers, wouldn't have to wait on hold for over an hour "due to unusually high call volumes" after your "AI" BOT provides no help every time we call your service team regardless of the time, day of the week, or month we are forced to call you.

Reason 2: The graphic was a good excuse to include pictures of cute kitties from my family in the book—no other reason necessary.

Returning to reason one. Your job is to first determine where you are going to be on the operational continuum. From this point establish the overall metrics and then make it part of every person's work objectives. Maybe you still won't get anything done but at least you will save countless arguments at team meetings. There are worse alternatives such as paying for consultants and expensive quality improvement projects that never achieve anything other than digging a deeper hole you must climb out of.

What do you do first? How about if we start with what NOT to do regarding operational improvement:

- Do not think that improvement requires some kind of mystic religious experience that requires the high priestess of the Fat Eight Omega process methodology to come in and bestow a whole new level of bureaucracy. This is just fluff added to either fool clients or executives following them. The most likely reason is the boss is demonstrating that they are "doing something" about an operational problem.

- Do not bring in enterprise consultants to give you the answers. The good news is that in many cases your competition is just as incompetent as you are. In today's world this means they are also using the same consultants that provide the same formulas to allegedly improve team performance as they are giving you. If you believe a recent twenty-four-year-old college graduate from an alleged elite school, but who has never successfully executed a real business plan, has some magical operational knowledge please re-read Chapter Two for the real root cause of your problems. You will not like what team leader category you are in.

- Run ads and tell your clients that quality is your #1 priority. It won't fool your current clients. It won't convince your past customers. I guess you are looking for future customers to bad-mouth you and leave as soon as possible due to your lack of quality and integrity.

If these are ineffective strategies, why are they the first things team executives do when addressing perceived operational issues? Do you have to ask? They are simplistic and require little critical thinking. These are the two crown jewels in the holy grail of many executive decision-making processes. Establishing real operational metrics and insisting that everyone follow them is hard work and costs money. If the boss isn't requiring hard work and you aren't getting rewarded for this work, why would anyone think it is going to get done? The second reason is what a great way to pretend you are addressing operational concerns while refusing to acknowledge your real goal is delivering a low-quality operational model. Do you think your team members are really fooled? Your customers? If you are serious about improving your operational metrics review the following steps.

CREATE REAL OPERATIONAL METRICS

While it sounds simple, creating real operational metrics are not done. IT doesn't get done because the leaders really don't require IT. IT is hard, and IT may expose some people who are considered great performers as the team boat anchors they are. Instead of doing IT, why not crank out that quality presentation showing you are "doing something" about IT? Anything but "IT."

Who needs to create operational metrics for their team? Talk to many people in team leadership positions and they will say they know in their gut if someone is doing a good job. Maybe this is true. The more likely scenario is your "gut" is really a mishmash of what you have digested in the past, i.e., random thoughts and memories you sift through around appraisal time. That disgusting chicken sandwich from Joe's Gas and Chicken Shack you ate last month remains a memory long after that delicious chicken sandwich you had last week at your favorite restaurant, Le Château d'Hélène. For my vegan friends, please use nut patty and veggie free-range lettuce sandwich in the preceding sentence.

Since you can't grasp anything good or bad someone did, then human nature kicks in and you default to feelings. Do I like their personality? Do I understand what they do? Do they bother me? By the way, "they don't bother me" is the most tempting metric of all for a busy team manager. "Just shut up and do your job" seems like an excellent metric on a team full of whiners doesn't it? Then after you get in touch with your feelings proceed to work backwards to justify the feelings with metrics to support it. Sometimes you get lucky and hit the bull's-eye identifying a good metric. Other times the bull just hits the team.

The other problem for managers is that metrics are just hard work.

Remember in Chapter 3 we discussed why many managers become managers. Hard work was not in the top ten reasons to be on the list. In fact, not sure that is on any manager's list of reasons for taking a leadership position. I am assuming that if you are reading this book, you are not one of them. This means you are making an attempt at real team leadership and will recall both the importance of metrics and how much WORK it will take to create them in most organizations. If you delegate the hard work of creating metrics to a tool jockey, e.g., productivity software or department, you usually get more bad behaviors. It is in the best interest of the tool department to make things as complicated as possible to ensure their long-term employment and gain more organizational power. It is also in the best interest of a software company to make sure you are as dependent on "upgrades" and custom coding work as well.

Much like a government department budget either "solution" will just get bigger and more expensive. While it was easy it is no longer cheap. The good news, at least for the team leader using this approach, is it enables the manager to abdicate responsibility for operational issues and point to the quality department if there are no improvements. The tool is bad, complicated, or doesn't measure the right thing. This keeps the game going for years. Again, the more you can blur accountability and responsibility the better if your goal is achieving a personal team empire.

Cast off the goal of blurring accountability and create legitimate metrics that will give you an accurate indication of the direction you are going. This is where the right metrics are created that determine company success and have been defined and translated into everyone's individual performance metrics. If you use surveys as part of your operational metrics ensure they ask the right questions, measure the right metrics, and are given to the right people. You can't use just one metric such as customer surveys. Remember, a survey is just a feeling at the second a particular human is answering the question. Surveys are overused for the reasons mentioned above. Cheap, easy, and everyone says how important they are. While determining how your customers perceive your products and services is important, surveys must be balanced with other operational metrics that are required for your team to be successful. The most important component of all is the ability to explain to the team members how these components directly impact the success of the company and team as well as their personal success.

PUBLISH

You have the key metrics in place now? Here is a novel idea. Tell everyone ahead of time what you are considering. Publish them. Enable members of the team to question the metrics and provide feedback on their validity. Then really go crazy and tell everyone on the team how the entire team will be measured against those metrics as well as how this will be used in any bonus structure as each individual team defines their individual bonus structure for team members.

The amazing part about this is how many leaders say they do publish their objectives. On a surface level it might be true. There are many organizations that publish the high-level financials and goals. However, when this cascades down the organization, they become increasing vague, aspirational like "core values," or self-created allegedly based on higher vague goals like customer satisfaction.

MEASURE

Oh no, you mean we aren't done yet? Yes, now is the time for even more hard work that involves honest measurement of the published metrics.

102 | THERE IS AN i IN TEAM

If a team sees the measurement is fair and used for the entire team it brings credibility to the entire process. People may not agree, but if they know the measurement it clears the way to enforcing good team behavior. If you deviate from honest measurement, you are destroying credibility and team motivation to achieve goals going forward. Honesty and integrity in measurement is the only thing that will sustain improvement. Your high-performing people have heard broken promises their entire working life and will assume you won't follow through either. Your new employees will also be demotivated when they discover you don't follow through. When you do follow through you buy respect and credibility, even from those who may disagree with your approach.

REWARD

Operational metrics at the company level should be translated into each level below, right down to the individual. As discussed in the previous chapter on financial objectives, the same effort placed on adding financials to the bonus program should also be done with operational considerations. Every bonus program must have both to make the bonus real at both the team level and distributed to the individual performer. If you just have a team goal you have failed. There are too many people in the world willing to be carried across the finish line by the team. Only when you have the individuals incented to achieve their operational goals can you move to achieving the team goals. Rewards should work both ways. You should have negative rewards as well as positive rewards for behavior and results.

TEAMWORK MOMENT OF TRUTH
When all is said and done, much is said and little is done.

Stop talking about it. Stop having team classes. Stop hiring alleged experts and start doing something about teamwork by implementing meaningful operational metrics and start measuring success. While you are creating the metrics make sure you are not only measuring the right thing but asking the right people the right questions. Hey that was easy, but wait a minute, what kind of metrics did you put into place?

Unfortunately, instead of good operational metrics team leaders usually create metrics that fall into one of three easy-to-categorize metric buckets:

- No Metrics.
- Stupid Metrics.
- Good Metrics Gone Bad.

NO METRICS

This is where the team leader just knows when you are doing a good job. Conversely, you will also find out eventually if the boss thinks you are doing a poor job as well. This means your raises are based purely on perception at the time of the performance appraisal. Even if you use no metrics, at least tell people you don't have them. A more typical no metric is when an employee walks into a performance appraisal having no idea what the basis is for their performance rating. They have a perception of what their job is: Answer the phone, fix the computer equipment, complete the project tasks, but after that good luck. Usually, most of the team makes up their own metrics because nature abhors a vacuum. Good people will typically attempt to guess well and work hard at it. Smart, but not necessarily good, team members will spend more time attempting to figure out how to game the system. One great way to receive high scores is by demonstrating loyalty and just agreeing with everything the boss says. The best tactic is to laugh at all her jokes.

The worse type of no metrics is where the company requires you to build your goals, assign percentages, and adds categories around nebulous items such as values. Then at the performance appraisal you hit all the agreed-to goals and the boss says, "yes, but it doesn't feel like you performed so I lowered your performance rating." If your team leader is really a coward, you will get good ratings on achieving the business goals and then get rated low on Human Resource-inserted categories such as "effective team building" or "business acumen." Consider the irony of a dysfunctional boss giving out business acumen ratings.

STUPID METRICS

Oh no! Your boss went to a training class and was told that a good leader establishes metrics to build high-performance work teams. OK, if a boss needs a training class in establishing metrics chances are you will get something worse than no metrics, you typically will get stupid metrics. If the boss is really bad you will get uber stupid metrics. If your metrics are not tied to the overall team metrics, what appears to be a good individual metric will transform into a good-looking stupid metric.

A real-life example I witnessed is what happened when one team in one division needed important information. Metrics were created to ensure the data was acquired, and how it impacted the entire organization. Here's how it started: After every service call technicians were supposed to complete a paper activity report. Management never told the technicians what these were going to be used for, just that they were required to be filled out and submitted. Reporting by the technicians was sketchy at best. Since no one had told them what the reports were for, or acted like they were important, they were the last thing on the technicians' "to do" list. But here's the important background. The secret reason the activity reports were created was for the product team to receive data to determine how the equipment in the field performed; others wanted reporting on activities the field service teams around the world were doing back at the home office.

Since there was only a twenty percent response rate at best on paper data and the information provided was poor, it was determined there was only one way to get better reporting from the field: automation! Technicians were trained, millions of dollars in wireless handheld data entry units purchased, and supporting technology was deployed. A data warehouse was then created, and millions of dollars were spent on implementation, reporting, and training. Finally, we will have data that is a click away to make informed decisions about the business! We also could now collect data with incredible speed. As shocking as this sounds, the first thing everyone noticed was that the data was as sketchy in the database with the wireless devices as it was with the paper reports. Product complained and the executive in charge of service finally decided to fix the problem and put an operational metric in place. The technicians were ordered to account for 40 hours a week working on a customer's technical problem or be written up.

Everyone got the message. Let the law of unattended consequences begin! Of course, the technicians possessed all the serial numbers of the assigned equipment and each Friday selected equipment and randomly assigned work hours to ensure the forty-hours goal was reported. Some of the ambitious performers did it each day as opposed to waiting until the end of the week. The team leader achieved the metric, the home office was happy, and the database was chock full of data. Once again, this seemed to prove that creating metrics, publishing, measuring, and rewarding certainly works.

The only problem was the original reason to even do these tickets. The product team had the crazy idea to use this data to make important long-term decisions on product performance. This report was provided to the product team to determine how the overall product reliability was across all models to send back to the manufacturing plants around the world. It was also used to set maintenance rates for all equipment and determine technician workload of different computers and peripheral models, which in turn determined head count projections for each area. Profitability of product lines was impacted by "low quality" products due to number and length of the service calls. In addition, no one questioned how it was even possible to have a 100% productivity level for technicians working on service calls. It was precisely the opposite. Managers were being rewarded for increasing "productivity" due to their leadership skills.

After multiple complaints, the service management team validated the reason they were promoted to a leadership position. They paid consultants to figure out what the problem was; they determined the metrics needed to be defined. A new metric was published; it stated you must have 80% of productive hours against repair and can't have the same serial number in the same week or that would count against a technician as a return repair. The response from the technical team is easy to determine. Technicians just kept a list of all serial numbers assigned to them and picked different serial numbers on each call to ensure they were not "dinged" by a return repair call. They then used thirty-two hours instead of forty hours to arrive at their targeted weekly number. Once again, success in achieving the operational metric. Unless you count all this combined team dysynergy effort as productive work, what have you accomplished to improve team performance?

The product development group got the data they wanted. Now it looked like repairs of certain equipment models took three hours instead of the half-hour anticipated when setting prices. Poor quality means high service cost, which meant raising maintenance rates on equipment. The service team executives also got the data they wanted, which was increased productivity and reporting from the worldwide service team due to their strategic decisions. Then after realizing the products were no longer competitive, they determined that the data was bad. Instead of looking at the root cause, which is hard and would have also required calling out the service team for bad data, they had simply mandated a twenty percent reduction in the hours reported and discarded other reporting data that didn't fit their projections for a product. This compounded the errors in reporting. Some units were breaking frequently, causing customer complaints and lost revenue from warrantee and maintenance contracts, while other units were performing better yet sunset early due to perceived quality issues.

The consequences of these types of decisions are usually not felt right away. In this case the data led to yearly increases in new system pricing and maintenance rates, which caused many customers to cancel maintenance contracts and go on a time and material service basis, since the equipment they had rarely went down. In some cases, price increases led to a drop in satisfaction and moving to a competitor. Forget a quality circle. This is the circle of quality dysfunctionality!

TEAMWORK MOMENT OF TRUTH

Metrics get the results you think you are looking for, not necessarily what you should be looking for.

The moral of this story is that all the metrics in the world will not matter if all the teams are not aligned to the overall goals and objectives of the organization. If each team creates metrics, they may look "good" at the team level, however, they look very stupid when viewed as a tactic to achieve the overall goals of the organization.

GOOD METRICS GONE BAD— THE CUSTOMER SURVEY

There are metrics that sound good on a presentation until you look a little closer. You then discover a good general metric that has been turned into a bad or even uber stupid and bad metric. At the front of the line is the holy grail of operational metrics—the revered customer survey. This is the favorite operational metric in use today. There is data that suggests that utilized the right way the customer survey can be a component of your operational metrics. Unfortunately, the only reason it has been embraced by many teams is that it fosters the illusion of a hard metric. It is cheap, easy to deploy, and most importantly easily manipulated.

There have been many books written and thousands of research hours performed on customer surveys. What questions to ask, how to statistically rank them, even creating allegedly new breakout measurement methodologies such as net promoter score that will lead you to the customer satisfaction promised land. Once again, human nature trumps scientific survey analysis as this is just another attempt at a dismal science. The great thing about customer satisfaction surveys is how easy they can be manipulated and/or misunderstood. What is customer satisfaction? Does your team really want to know if the customer is satisfied and if they do know, satisfied with what? Do you care if you are rated 10 out of 10 or if they buy from you again? If they buy from you again, will it be because you scored high on a measured survey based on a buying event? Is the person answering the survey telling the truth? Is it the right person taking the survey? The methodology and analysis of questions become even more complicated when you are attempting to use surveys in a B-to-B (Business to Business) environment as opposed to end customers.

If I am told my individual operational metric and rating will be based on how my customer fills out a survey, what happens? I have two options:

Option 1: The survey will motivate me to drive my organization to provide the service my customer is expecting.

Option 2: Since option one is out of my control, do everything I can to have my customer fill the survey out about only me. As a risk mitigation strategy ensure I have gathered enough evidence to blame other internal teams or external factors for the survey results. This is much more effective if you can build the case prior to the survey scores to set the appropriate expectations with the senior team leaders. Of course, this option is only used if the results are bad. If they are good results, you can take credit for overcoming the other support team's failure to provide good service.

Does anyone want to guess what option is used for most customer surveys that are used for metrics, particularly in the B-to-B arena?

Here's an example of a great direct customer survey measurement that I was involved in. One day I pushed on the down button to lower the window on my relatively new car. With a terrible sound the window went down twice as fast, made a loud noise, and then would not open. I took the car to the dealership where I had bought it, for which I had an extended bumper-to-bumper warranty. This wasn't just any run-of-the-mill warranty. It was a Gold bumper-to-bumper warranty that covered everything right down to the buttons. When it was time to pick up the car I was presented with a repair bill. I asked my service "consultant" why I was charged since I had already paid for the bumper-to-bumper Gold service coverage. The service consultant explained that while the window motor was indeed the issue and covered, since the braking mechanism within the motor failed it also rammed the window so hard it cracked the glass at the point where the motor arm attached to the window. They had to replace the glass and as paragraph C subsection 4 in small print states, the warrantee doesn't cover glass breakage. He then proceeded to tell me the good news was they were giving me a discount on the window replacement.

After arguing and escalating with no success I finally gave up. Before I left the same guy who delivered the bad news asked me to fill out the client satisfaction card. He said his performance appraisal and job was dependent on getting a good rating. The only thing rated was whether he was courteous and answered my questions. I asked does it matter even if I didn't like your manager or dealership's response. He told me he was sorry but that's how it works; he is the only one who will be impacted if I send in a negative survey. I must give the service representative credit for honesty.

Now you know one of the reasons why car dealers get high customer satisfaction ratings on satisfaction surveys. It also masks different customer behaviors. I knew it wasn't really the service advisor's fault I was charged so I didn't want to give a 0 rating and get him in trouble. Therefore, I didn't fill out the survey at all. The bottom line, though, is that a $180 decision ended up costing the dealer tens of thousands in revenue. I never bought another car from them. At this point since that incident, we are now at six cars in a row purchased from other dealers. And I've never purchased another extended warrantee from a car dealer. I am also sure I influenced many others to reconsider both options as well when making a car buying decision. How much has paragraph C subsection 4 on cracked glass coverage really cost this "highly rated" dealership? To date, six new car purchases, and considerable word of mouth negative advertising telling this story to others.

Manipulating customer surveys happens all the time. Usually, it is not as straightforward as my experience with the car dealership, but it is still in place as soon as it is determined this easy measurement should be used as an operational objective. In a B-to-B survey other ways to manipulate the results are making sure only one contact at a company that is friends with a support person or sales gets the survey. Then there is asking the wrong questions, such as "is my account rep friendly and calls me back" as opposed to questions that uncover whether the product or service is considered valuable and is priced correctly. Surveys are also used to blame the messenger when a product fails to deliver and is overpriced. Blaming the account representative for a bad survey, as in the example at the car dealership, is prevalent on many so-called teams. After all, he should have "managed" my expectations to create a positive "experience" regarding the transaction.

The same monkey business that people use in creating "positive" financials to make everything look good is also used to show positive operational metrics in quality and customer survey ratings. If you are unwilling to measure accurately, attempt to gain insight, and then target how to improve performance, you will continue to fail while receiving excellent client satisfaction ratings. If the entire performance measurement is based on how much a customer likes the account representative you will usually get high ratings as the person with the metric works to control the results.

I have seen countless examples of a company getting five-star reviews from business customers over a couple of years followed by the company receiving notification that the customer isn't renewing their contract. Must be some other reason, right? Just keep on fooling yourself. The same trap can be applied to any operational metric you create. They look good but at the end of the day they turned out to be a bad indication of excellent operational performance.

GREAT METRICS ON FANTASY ISLAND

There are also the great metrics that will guarantee you a write up in a publication or business paper. The problem is that it isn't really a metric or worse is a fake metric such as being awarded greatest place ever to work in the history of the world. As if that goal was ever correlated to actual team performance. Everyone agrees to use the Fantasy Island Metrics as part of the process to measure performance and bonus. The only problem is those "metrics" don't measure performance and thus bonuses.

AUTOMATION AND METRIC EXTREMES

There is also a tendency if given enough data to go to extremes. On the one end there are the managers who rule by gut feelings, with no metrics or a few stupid metrics. Down the hall to the right there are team leaders who follow the other extreme of using hundreds of metrics. Why? Because in the age of automation you can. The problem is you lose focus on what the business is truly about, and business is really not that complicated. If you have twenty things you are attempting to measure, after a while you are just measuring the measurements. You may achieve nineteen metrics and declare success. Of course, the twentieth is lost sales, which could be construed as a bad thing, but the law of averages applies enabling you to declare victory. This may be an obvious example to many leaders, yet over time many fall into the trap of creating more and more metrics, which translates into creating all sorts of problems. Keep to three to five key metrics that are fed by just a few inputs, and you will begin to get an excellent snapshot of operational performance. The hard work is in determining the right things to measure.

TEAMWORK MOMENT OF TRUTH

The number of metrics that are created to address team performance doesn't fix performance. It is just an indicator of how many problems the team is having.

Customer focus and the long-term health of the organization are paramount. That translates into such things as are the customers "happy" enough to continue buying your service or products. Providing the right service and products enables the organization to make a profit and continue to create and sell new products and services. All your metrics need to be built around this. Sounds logical and self-evident, just like financial objectives, but look around and see how many organizations actually do this. This doesn't mean you should have a slide presentation that says you do this, or an advertising campaign.

You also may have massive spreadsheets from a database that enables you to take different surveys and perform extensive analytics using highly paid "data scientists" to demonstrate how seriously you take customer satisfaction. That is the easy part, despite what the Vice President of Client Happiness says. The hard part is how this translates into meaningful metrics. When you talk to individual team members, how many can articulate their objectives, how these impact their pay, and how they contribute to the success of the overall team?

Without good operational metrics things will go wrong and when they go wrong, since no one can articulate what the problem is, there is only one recourse. The executive leaders then define operational success by cutting costs by 20%. What if you lose 30% of your customers or the quality of the product is reduced, which lowers the potential of your team succeeding or even surviving in the future? In the end, you have an operational metric that is measurable and achievable.

How easy was that? Oh, it's not? Why not? This may be an opportune moment to ask if your operations leadership group doesn't grasp how to increase quality and efficiency, why they should be employed. Isn't that an integral part of "Operations?" If the answer to fixing their organization is bringing in a "quality" consultant, why don't you just hire the quality expert and dismiss the person requesting one? Real operational metrics are the key to team success. Nothing more complex than that.

You must decide where you need to be on the customer continuum to achieve the goal of long-term business operational sustainability. The good news is some of the additional cost of improving operational quality can be funded by eliminating the quality advertisements and posters as well as all those high-priced consultants who are creating programs for quality improvement. If you do improve in today's information age, word will get out quickly that you have turned things around. You can do this even if you have no credibility after your advertisements on your quality operations were ruined by news stories about your toaster causing bagels to explode and putting out a customer's eye. It will just take longer. A commitment to real operational improvement will bring you success in the marketplace. Unless of course the trial lawyers and state attorneys are successful in that class action lawsuit over your toaster.

If your idea of quality is to put out a sign that says, "at Widget World quality is job one," the odds are low that you are capable of making a quality product. Your team is just creating propaganda that will be seen through in a minute by your employees and two minutes later by your customers. If you believe posters work, I also can't believe you made it through Chapter 6 of this book. Now, on to the final and most difficult building block for building highly effective teams.

CHAPTER 7

BUILDING BLOCK #3: PEOPLE

"The problem with people is that they are only human."

BILL WATTERSON

Yes, your people are your MOST important asset. After all, you say it all the time and even have coffee mugs and posters to prove it. Of course, what is the first thing that gets thrown out of the building when the going gets tough and the company is in trouble? What?? You throw out your PEOPLE? Why not the power plant, your manufacturing line, or all your products? I think I know the answer.

TEAMWORK MOMENT OF TRUTH

Most people on your team are not your most important asset

OK, having a quote from the CEO in the annual report that says, 'Most of our people are not our most important asset,' is not great marketing, even though it is true. You still need to ask the question— What kind of individuals do I need and what kind do I have?

In the parlance of our current social media and turning everything into a binary good vs, evil discussion of any subject, consider this a Trigger Warning. If you are a true believer that your side is good and the other is evil, I suggest just skipping this chapter for your own mental health. It is entirely too nuanced for your mindset.

Did you leave yet? OK, we can now continue, since you have been warned. When it comes to the topic of what type of employees a team and/or the entire organization needs, there has been an almost universal message that has been emanating out of the vast majority of divisions that have names like Human Resources (HR), Talent, and People. I will use the acronym HR to represent all these entities moving forward, with apologies to the Chief People Officers running a division called Talent. From nearly all HR practitioners, who all attend the same HR seminars, and have the same college degrees and certifications, you will usually hear two universal answers on how to create great teams:

- We need engaged employees to create highly productive teams!

- Social engineering programs, because that creates even higher performing teams!

EMPLOYEE ENGAGEMENT

One of the ideas on creating a successful team that may have started out with good intentions is the concept of employee engagement, which is coupled with employee happiness. Do you really think everyone is going to be happy and engaged on your team? Ever? This translates into crazy ideas about making employees "happy" by creating a great work "culture." The challenge is that a great work culture for me may be a terrible work culture for thee. Is your goal to create a team culture where your lazy, unproductive slackers rate you as the best place to work in some magazine news feed because you have parties, "free" extra benefits, and low expectations? If your team members have the right characteristics and are in the right job, your organization can contribute to your team members becoming happy in their work. Having said that, without the right goals and metrics in place at the organizational level, how do you define how "happy" your employees should be?

An organization isn't in business to make you happy. You can partially attribute this to the steady drumbeat of the mass media and popular culture by people who don't understand human nature or what make teams work. Speaking of mass media and social media drumbeats, this leads me to the second topic.

SOCIAL ENGINEERING PROGRAMS

There is a trend to convince you that performance will improve if you invest a lot of money in various social engineering programs for your team. The names will constantly change over time, but the goals are the same. The current flavor falls under the umbrella of Diversity, Equity, and Inclusion, otherwise known by its acronym DEI. These types of programs always claim they will allegedly produce better outcomes without any solid evidence that it is true, other than saying it over and over. The people repeating this mantra include consultants, members of social "science" academia, and a variety of true believers. This in turn is echoed by unquestioning news outlets and social media influencers. Their proof that it is true is typically surveying people who are either in their academic or HR circle. This also includes highly paid executives in charge of these programs, consultants making hundreds of thousands of dollars to build and deliver these programs, and executives who have personal incentives to complete the surveys with gushing praise. Then there are the team members filling out surveys and who understand it is not in their best career interests to admit these programs didn't produce better operational results. Does anyone seriously think that most people in these organizations are going to tell the boss that these programs as currently being pushed have no evidence of improving actual team performance?

We live in a world where many people have abandoned a nuanced approach to concepts and ideas. Instead, what has been emanating out of our allegedly higher education institutions and now permeating throughout teams and society in general, is a binary good vs. evil framework. The result is when you disagree with how something is currently being framed you are automatically categorized in the most derogatory terms, and in some cases lose your employment based on your viewpoint. This has devolved into a decrease in open dialogue, decrease in effective teamwork, an increase in nonproductive bureaucracy, and a distraction from the entire reason the team was created to begin with. Of course, this is great when your team is "winning" but a pendulum tends to swing back the other way at some point. This is rarely a consideration in today's overall environment of good vs. evil.

If you have moved in this direction towards dogmatic belief in your cause, regardless of what side you are on, you are moving into dangerous territory for creating effective teams no matter how much you personally believe in a concept. There are many compelling reasons to promote diversity, create an inclusive work environment, and support equal treatment of people on teams and in organizations. I agree strongly that a case can be made that many teams can be more successful having a diversity of perspectives and skill sets to achieve goals. The challenge is we have started to confuse the diversity we need in skills, knowledge, and perspectives to be successful with a simplistic worldview of just defining diversity as based on just human physical appearances and an array of other behaviors that one could argue do not contribute to creating a successful team.

Another reason there should be a focus on this is ensuring team leaders and executives are not letting personal bias get in the way of hiring and/or promoting great candidates for the team. I have seen too many instances where someone is hired based on the individual bias of the team leader but the reasons are not related at all to team performance. Since the beginning of time humans have leveraged personal bias around things they find familiar. This includes such items as, does the person look like me, do they have the same background, same personality type, same hobbies, or are they the same sex as me? There is a history of using these personal biases to determine if the person is the "right" fit for their team. Apologies to the people who are looking for the binary of oppressors vs. victims, but no subclassification of humans that you want to shoehorn into a group is exempt from this type of behavior.

In today's world if you are excluding people from the team due to these personal biases, you are not focused on creating a better team. In the worst cases, I have witnessed people who were illegally discriminating against potentially great team members. These are the team leaders who should have never been promoted or hired to be a leader in the first place. The chances of changing this behavior with training or an executive seminar are slim to none. Review Chapter 3 again on the type of people who typically get promoted if you think a seminar will bring enlightenment to most of these characters.

Conversely, there are other people on your team who claim they are focused on ensuring we are not missing out on great talent while in the pursuit of other goals that are not focused on creating better teams. This includes gaining additional power within an organization by advocating and forcing programs on teams, which usually creates the opposite of the published goals. This creates a different set of biases where people are placed in positions and elevated for a variety of reasons that have nothing to do with their skills and performance. Then the leader implementing these programs gets to achieve their goals without showing any measurable improvement in team performance. In fact, the opposite occurs, as it destroys work teams like a slow poison as other members of the team see hires and promotions that are based on reasons that have nothing to do with running effective teams.

One thing that works better than any of these programs is understanding that for the most part humans like being associated with a winning team. There is a reason you see a great deal of dissension on a losing sports team no matter how hard the coach tries to build morale—they're losers. You can attempt to make your last-place team a fun place to work. You can even hang posters in the locker room that say, "We promote equity of outcomes" or "Diversity is our strength." How often does that work without having people who have the right talent and desire to be successful? If you don't have the right individuals, no amount of pre-season team training is going to get you to the championship game. You should be asking where are these people and how do you "get me some of that?"

SECRET INGREDIENTS
OF SUCCESSFUL PEOPLE

Now it's time to share the three secret ingredients of successful people who you should want on your team.

There are three things that every person in your organization must have to bring success and it's not a MX91C Certification or being a Purple Belt Process guru:

- Work Ethic.
- Goal Oriented.
- Take Accountability and Responsibility.

Weed out the people who don't have these three components and "magic" will start to happen in your organization.

Work Ethic

Every person hired must start with a work ethic. Work ethic does not discriminate based on race, country of origin, religion, age, or sexual orientation. It is the secret to your success. Who is someone with a work ethic? It is someone who believes that work is an integral part of their life. Work is not something they just do to get money to pursue other interests. With a work ethic, part of your self-esteem and worth is tied to work. Part of your mental composition is when you do a job you are committed to doing it right. You should know who in each of your work areas has a strong work ethic and it should not a secret on each team either. Some dismiss these people as workaholics.

This points to a lack of understanding regarding what work ethic is. There is a big difference between working to contribute to the success of the team and clocking in hours AT work. There are also many so-called "work alcoholics" who spend many hours at work doing nothing for work that is productive—at least for your team. Having a vice president who arrives every day at five-thirty in the morning and who brags he is the last to leave is not the metric you are looking for to define a good work ethic. Especially when the to-do list consists of eating breakfast, checking social media sites, clipping fingernails, taking two-hour lunches, and arguing with his wife on the phone for an hour. If that sounds like a personal experience about an allegedly workaholic boss as retold by a certain author, you are correct. Yes, time for another obvious teamwork moment of truth that appears to elude many team leaders.

> ### TEAMWORK MOMENT OF TRUTH
>
> Just because members of the team are AT work doesn't mean they are doing your team's work.

Having team members who possess a work ethic is not enough to make your organization a success. Otherwise, Mary in Information Technology who runs the fantasy football league or Robert in Marketing who sells cooking utensils for additional income would be the must-have people on every team. If your hard worker is attempting to achieve something pertaining to the nature of the team that is providing the paycheck, then you are on the right track.

Goal Oriented

Hire people who appreciate goals and strive to achieve them. People who are frustrated with this concept are not good employees, E-V-E-R. Send them to your competitor to hire because of their vast "technical knowledge." Despite what your HR department tells you, just getting through college should not be considered achieving much of a goal. Does anyone really believe that mommy and/or daddy paying for someone to attend college right after high school to get that playground supervising degree, with a minor in adult beverage overconsumption, offers must-have skills for the team? The only time showing up at school for four years should even be considered a goal achievement is when there is some real significance attached to it. First, was an actual skill learned that is required for the success of your team? Did the prospective team member consistently score good grades in meaningful classes? This does not include Marxist Didacticism or Snowboarding 102. Can a prospective team member provide other evidence of a work ethic in college? Did they go to school as an adult while working and achieved their education as a goal? Did they demonstrate any leadership abilities at school? How many classes did they take that directly apply to what the new team member's role calls for? Positive responses to any of these questions and then you can start to get interested in that educational piece of paper.

If the job candidate also did other things during their college years that show self-motivation and initiative that may be a trigger to become even more interested. These are also the type of people who will be drawn to your company once the word gets out that you reward people based on actual goal achievement. They will see your metrics, understand them, and get satisfaction from achieving those targets.

Of course, these goals need to be based on our basic Financial and Operational building blocks. If not, people will set their own goals, including finding their next job. The others will stay to work on goals such as improving their golf game, engage in excessive self-promotion four hours a day to get the next position on the ladder, or talk you into developing some custom software based on a new programming language for the express purpose of padding their resume for future employment opportunities. Of course, that never happens on your team, does it?

Accountability and Responsibility

There are people who always avoid being accountable for their actions and taking responsibility for outcomes. Some spend half of their time at work making sure they won't be blamed and the other half making sure everyone else is blamed. I have seen this even when there are absolutely no consequences to admitting they were wrong. This behavior can be seen up and down an organization, including by CEOs who refuse to believe their own actions have created any problems. It must have been the lack of execution on the part of 10,000 other team members.

There are people in the world who just can't accept responsibility for their efforts on the job, let alone take accountability for the outcomes. I have worked with, for, and had people report to me who would rather chew off their right arm than to ever admit they had any part in the failure of a task or project. These people naturally gravitate to organizations that accept this type of behavior for a variety of reasons. This is also why many people love the team concept. If the team is responsible, it makes accountability softer. By blaming "the team" you are sentencing people who did above and beyond work to make your ridiculous idea successful to rise or sink with people who did not pull their own weight. The poor performing employee may lose 20% of their bonus, but they didn't care about that to begin with. They have other priorities, such as the upcoming fantasy football draft. Is this who you want on your "team?"

If you take a team survey, everyone including chiefs, vice presidents, directors, managers, all the way through groundskeeper, may have an opinion as to who is accountable for what. One must be careful regarding what it means to be accountable, otherwise the process guys will come in and create process flows down to the last email confirmation as to who does what. This creates a crippling effect as people ensure, or at least attempt to ensure, that nothing can be pointed at them for the reason behind any failure. If you disagree, perhaps you skimmed over the Chapter Three discussion on human nature.

PTA—PEOPLE TO AVOID

Now that you have the three basic ingredients in successful people, let's look at the types of people who tend to slip by the screening process when hiring and promoting because they are perceived as having the qualities needed for good team members: the expert, the loyalist, and the personal brand builder.

Experts

Sometimes teams tolerate certain behavior because they believe they need "experts." Since experts are hard to find one must make allowances for bad behavior. This could be someone who has considerable knowledge in a field or knows how to get things done in a large organizational bureaucratic structure through networking. No expert is worth this and no expert should be that important. If they are on your "team" I suggest asking yourself why. You may have just identified a fundamental flaw in the long-term viability of your organization. Secondly, experts with a bad attitude may appear to save the day in one area while usually creating roadblocks and demotivators in many other endeavors. The sad thing is most team leaders know who they are, set up different rules for them, and reap the negative consequences with all their other team members because they have convinced themselves that life won't go on if the "expert" leaves. People driven by a desire for company success and motivated by metrics are worth more than any expert at the high end of the market and who spend time doing things counter to the goals of the team.

Knowledge through Credentialed Experts

What defines an expert? If you are letting certifications or degrees dictate the expert tag, you are really in trouble. There is a high probability that your credentialed expert is a faux expert. They are beautiful on the outside but fake and unproductive on the inside. Sounds harsh; however, look at most certification processes. In general, most involve taking classes and passing tests, and oh yes, paying a fee. Yes, you may have to have a degree or "prove" (along with your financial institution's routing and transit number) that you have done work in the field. Does that really prove the person has the three key attributes required to achieve results?

How can you determine if the candidate has ever really, successfully done what the credential says they can do? Human Resource departments also love credentials because it is an easy and "scientific" way to score a job description pay scale. It is also way easier to load degrees and certifications required into an AI search engine to weed out candidates. Yet there is little actual real-world evidence that people with credentials bring any additional value over reading a few of books on a subject. The people who usually object to the preceding statement are employees in HR and people who spend time earning multiple alphabet credentials, usually at the company's expense. Then they adorn their credentials on their business titles, email signatures, and social media.

TEAMWORK MOMENT OF TRUTH

If you believe certifications lead to great teamwork, the only certification you have is one for insanity.

Let your competitors care about the importance of having people with advanced degrees and certifications and who possess an entitlement mentality. You're looking for smart people who demonstrate a commitment to excellence with a proven track record of success. If something needs to be learned, real experts will go learn it. You don't have to ask them to learn, they just learn it. If a new skill is needed, they will acquire it. If a team member needs help, they will lend a hand. This is worth more than a team of credential chasers. You know who these people are and if you don't the people who work for you can point them out. Yet this fundamental building block is paid lip service and then ignored. Dedicated people with proven records are passed over because "market rates" dictate a "credentialed" person needs to be in a position regardless of their ability to get things done or work for the benefit of the company. That's why most highly successful businesses in the last one-hundred years were started and run by PhDs and certified process black belts. Wait a minute, should I check the numbers on that again and get back to you, or do you already know the answer?

Using credentials is also a good way to avoid "blame" for a bad hire by managers and attempting to avoid the risk of hiring a person who doesn't work out. The only reason it is a true risk is because the manager doesn't have the metrics or the competence to fire someone when she recognizes she made a mistake in hiring. Instead, she covers her bet by hiring someone with credentials. It is also a safe risk mitigation strategy. You won't be blamed if the new hire fails. After all you hired someone from Harvard with a MCDPEOS. How could it be your fault they were a total failure?

I'm not saying people with credentials should be avoided or their accomplishments not considered. I'm just suggesting that some of your alphabet soup-credentialed people may not have acquired the credentials to become more knowledgeable or to assist your team in improving performance.

Company Loyalist

Conversely, inside people are promoted solely because they have been there forever, and it is "their turn" as a reward for loyalty to the company or boss. They have been doing the job for such a long time it is assumed they must know how to do it and can move to the next level. The Peter Principle, articulated by Laurence J. Peter, states that in organizations people tend to rise to their level of incompetency. It is amazing that after all the years and all the alleged knowledge we have accumulated about managing teams that this simple truth is even more prevalent today than ever. Unfortunately, Mr. Peter was wrong. On most teams an employee can easily move two or more levels up before it becomes obvious to everyone but the clueless that this person is incompetent.

Without good metrics a vice president may be someone who has "charisma," the CEO likes him, or is able to deflect "blame" to other organizations. This may be considered a valuable asset by the boss while the three-hundred people reporting to these people find them absolutely incompetent. This disconnect on defining incompetence and the value of people relates directly back to the lack of accountability through financial and operational metrics as well as the reason many of these people end up as team leaders to begin with. How can you determine if you even have the right people in place until you put those metrics into practice across all levels?

Personal Brand Builders

What once was called shameless employee self-promotion has somehow been given a new name and become an acceptable part of some organizations. The latest name is Personal Brand Building. In addition to sounding much better than shameless self-promotion, brand builders can cross key areas of PTA competencies to deliver the kind of value only a highly incompetent team leader could hope for. They are easy to identify with just a simple search of social media sites. Their goal is for people to recognize them for, well, just recognizing them. The amazing thing is in some cases you can notice by reading their posts, re-posts, and activities they are doing how little time they are spending doing the work you hired them to do.

> **TEAMWORK MOMENT OF TRUTH**
>
> If you believe PTA (People to Avoid) characteristics are what good looks like in employees, you might be an LTA (Leader to Avoid)

Without the appropriate accountability metrics in place, a majority of your current team members could be roadblocks as opposed to building blocks to success. You may find that 75% of your employees do not have the right stuff due to twenty years of hiring the wrong stuff. The good news is even if 75% of the staff were hired for the wrong reason that doesn't mean they can't change. Many have just settled for this level of performance because that is what was demanded. You absolutely can rekindle the light in many of them. Put the metrics in place, raise the bar, demand excellence, and you will be amazed how many of your people start to get it. The key is you can't start with people. You must start with the first two building blocks in place. If all the people reporting to a person in a leadership role thinks a person on the team is incompetent and you don't, it can only be one of two reasons:

1. The person is incompetent at their job.

2. All the employees have no idea how good the boss is due to not wanting to take any accountability, stupidity, and/ or lack of awareness.

JACK'S CIRCLE OF TEAM
DYSFUNCTIONALITY CONUNDRUM

Chances are the reason is 1; and if it is 2, they are right anyway because you should have already fired all of them if 1 wasn't true.

People, not nebulous teams, are the ingredient that will take whatever the mission is and make it more powerful. The key is defining that mission and the financial and quality objectives required before you can claim your people are the "best." Your competitors all have the same problem as you do. Most are locked into old methods and ways of thinking. By investing in the right people, and consistently looking at how to improve processes, products, and procedures, you will create enormous opportunities.

These three people ingredients—Work Ethic, Goal Oriented, and Accountability—are "must haves" if you want success. Hire people with these three ingredients, establish goals and objectives, compensate them for performance, and watch your company grow. The next thing you know Harvard will be doing business cases on your company as people marvel at how successful your methodologies, IT systems, HR programs, business models, and organizational charts" are the latest golden tickets to success. Just make sure your competitors don't find out the real reason. Tell everyone you installed multimillion dollar supply chain software and used high-priced consultants with eight omega methodologies that fixed everything. Then laugh as you watch your competitors attempt to duplicate your success only to see their operational expenses grow, making your products and services even more compelling in the marketplace.

CHAPTER 8

WHERE ARE YOU NOW? TEAM MATURITY

"Denial ain't just a river in Egypt."

MARK TWAIN

N ow you know the three ingredients to a successful team, or should I say, now you remember the three original ingredients to a successful team: Excellent financial and operational objectives followed by great people with the right stuff. You also recognize that your team needs to change, and you are ready to make it happen. Hold on. Before attempting to fix any team, especially if you are new to the organization, you need to determine where your team is in terms of maturity. Knowing the maturity of both your individuals as well as the teams they belong to will assist you in developing your plan to change team culture and help achieve your goals faster. Many executives are completely disconnected from the real culture and maturity of their various teams. Then again, there are many executives who are the primary reason the team has such a dysfunctional culture to begin with.

TEAMWORK MOMENT OF TRUTH

Dysfunctional teams are never fixed by dysfunctional leaders. The problem is dysfunctional leaders don't think they are dysfunctional.

MATURITY MODELS

From an analysis perspective it is fascinating how many teams can function with different maturity levels across an entire organization. A CEO and half of the executive team may be at a high maturity level and assume that all the teams are following the lead of the CEO. There may be one division leader who talks about how her team is at a high maturity level. The problem is just a few interactions may demonstrate her organizational team behavior doesn't reflect her words. Individuals and teams can be generally placed in the following maturity models:

- Grade School.

- High School.

- Adult Education: Autodidact (Self-learners).

Yes, I could have come up with some fancy term like Organizational Quantitative Maturity Terateamism, and if you are a consultant, I am copywriting the word right now and expect future compensation for this game-changing process analysis concept. Instead of adding more awesomeness to our overinflated business vocabulary, why not state reality? These three groups are certainly not age dependent. Watching a forty-year-old throw a chair at a business meeting was all it took for me to understand that age doesn't really have much to do with a person's individual or team maturity classification. It is now time to join me in a trip back to your educational past and realize how some of the worst moments are alive and well in the allegedly mature adult team environment.

Grade School Teams

These are teams where the individuals exhibit the behavior of children. The key indicators are typically short-term focus, very self-centered, emotionally unstable, and the display of a complete lack of knowledge in the fundamentals of business or just playing well with others. The team doesn't have to demonstrate all four behaviors to qualify for grade school. For example, an overabundance of emotional instability more than compensates even if you have knowledge in the fundamentals of business. Before some of you team leaders get upset because you have perfect children, I'm sure your precious little angels don't act that way. For the purposes of this argument, just assume we are talking about those awful kids down the street.

Everything is near term with teams in grade school. There is no regard for the future because the future isn't here yet. Who needs long-term planning when you are having fun in the park right now? If you are not having fun, it must be someone else's fault. The other team has better toys, a better sandbox, and gets more attention from their mom, i.e., the boss. Did the stock double over last quarter? Why? That's an easy question since it doubled because of me. Since it was me there is no reason the value won't double again. There is not much time spent on analysis because you are living in the moment. Your future, just like a six-year-old's, will be much the same as today. Just get up and head for the playground.

There are several schools of thought that claim short-term goals work in business by focusing on just the next quarter results. Quarterly results at least take you from a six-year-old to a ten-year-old outlook on life. This type of "best practice" helps rationalize a grade school leader's view that short term is the only term. There is also an assumption that a mature adult can't focus on both short- and long-term goals. When this is the team focus at the top of the organization it encourages grade school team behavior at all levels of an organization. Short-term-only grade school teams also draw short-term immature investors to play in their sand box, and they demand next-day results as well. This usually ends badly when the sandbox value decreases because no one anticipated rain closing the sandbox one weekend. Adults focusing on both the short term and the long term recognize the good times won't last forever. The grade school team doesn't demonstrate that quality and can always rationalize failure by blaming others.

In addition to short-term-focus-only results, there is also a focus on toys. While teams are not asking for dolls and toy trucks, there are plenty of other toys that are "needed." Game rooms, office gyms, pool tables, and then the really big toys, such as buildings, company jets, and acquiring other companies. Instead of focusing on improving the current sandbox environment and toys the grade school executive just cries, I'm bored, I want a new toy to play with. And what could be a better toy than a new acquisition? Instead of focusing on improving business process execution, which may take some time to implement, including removing poor performers, they go for the quick fix.

A project team can't be successful unless it has some sort of enterprise software tool to collaborate or maybe a change agent consultant is hired to put the company through training. There, glad we were able to fix the problems with our team. This focus does make you wonder how they ever built anything in the "olden days." The Great Wall of China, the Empire State Building, the atomic bomb, and the pyramids were developed without a collaborative software project management tool, but you can't develop a marketing plan for a new broom without it? You don't need much of a business plan to justify acquiring a toy. Just say the magic word—synergy—and all your dreams come true. Whether it's falling in love with doing mergers because it is super exciting, or entering new lines of business that you know as much about as an eight-year-old, it doesn't matter. I want it now.

The reason a team gets away with being this type of company is usually in a market with no competitors or even better, no customers. Many startups with heavy investment from venture capitalists or some software development firms are great examples. Quality financials don't matter, team building social events and egocentric behavior are the norm. A team may even appear to be financially successful temporarily. A poor performing grade school can stay in business for years, especially if their competition is another grade school down the street. No one stops to consider how it could be twice as successful, and even put the other grade school out of business, if they ran the team like adults. Unlike a real grade school where we try the "no child left behind" theory, most of these companies either graduate, get acquired, or fail at some point.

We don't let our children make important decisions, or at least you shouldn't. If that is the case, why do we think these kids don't need adult supervision? Usually there is absolutely no hope for a long-term future here if this is the culture at the very top. Either the crash happens or the team graduates to another level. If you are on the board of directors or just became CEO of Team Grade School Inc., then there is hope. There is an excellent chance that if you can help the team grow up many of your employees will respond favorably.

I have witnessed situations where a startup CEO had the benefit of some wise advisors to help them on their journey of avoiding the pitfalls of turning to an inward-focused adult day care center. You can then move to a true adult organization of professionals. If only some teams within the organization demonstrate these characteristics as opposed to the entire organization, there is still hope for change. If you are put in charge of one of these "teams," chances are good that while you can't change everyone, changing some of the individuals will help bring success. If you are a team member in this type of environment with six-year-olds leading the team right up to the top, consider planning to graduate with or without the rest of the team.

High School Teams

Everyone is in a high school clique on the team. Only the names have changed. Information Technology, Sales, Finance, and HR teams have one goal: their group advancement. No one really cares about the school except maybe the public relations department, aka cheerleaders. Actually, sometimes they don't really care; they just want it to appear that they care and that everyone appears to have team spirit. The only thing that keeps things under control is if there is some adult supervision from the executive management team, i.e., the principal and assistant principals. If most of the management team are really the clique leaders who encourage loyalty to just their "team," you have an extremely dysfunctional high school. Friendship is the highest goal to achieve with the football quarterback, coolest kid, or other anointed ones. Do you get invited to the right parties, i.e., meetings or golf events? Team members are also like teenagers; you have things all figured out. You know exactly what the other clique should be doing and think your parents, i.e., your boss, is stupid. Your team does function on occasion; it is just difficult to figure out what level it could function at if everyone acted like adults.

You also have the team cheerleading squads. Even if everyone in the stands appears apathetic at best, this group constantly comes up with new cheers to get the troops motivated. Other cliques become even more demotivated by this. What software developer doesn't love to get a coffee mug that says "You're the Best" after spending 60 hours a week making a deadline happen only to have the project canceled without explanation? This goes right to fake team building. Get out the pom-poms and make everyone on the team excited. Put everyone in team training and then ask them if it worked. This creates real personal challenges for the adults who are stuck in this high school musical rerun as they attempt to navigate the High School Team Training acceptance process.

TEAMWORK MOMENT OF TRUTH

Team training provides one benefit. For the first time it unites the team with a shared sense of community: They all hate your team training program.

A sense of dread comes over you as you see the email that exclaims, "Exciting News from Human Resources!" in the header. You open the email to find the announcement with great fanfare of an exciting new MANDATORY Team Building Program. The process is described as a great way to ensure not only improved productivity, but enabling teams to bond and become excited about synergistic teamwork. In real life, the process is slightly more sobering than this cheerful picture of positive results. I've created a Team Training Process slide that more accurately reflects what's likely to happen—unlike the amazing outcomes your consultant promises if you deploy their "game-changing" training program.

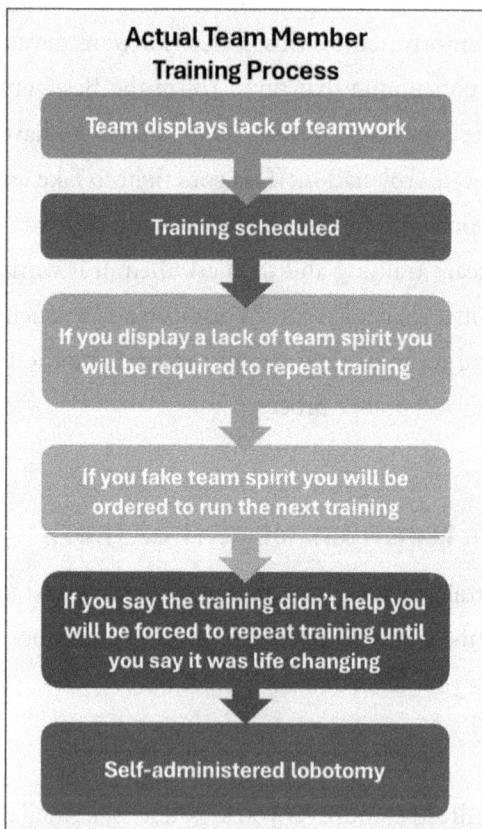

Actual Team Member Training Process

- Team displays lack of teamwork
- Training scheduled
- If you display a lack of team spirit you will be required to repeat training
- If you fake team spirit you will be ordered to run the next training
- If you say the training didn't help you will be forced to repeat training until you say it was life changing
- Self-administered lobotomy

As you can see from the above "peer reviewed" (by my co-workers) training process, there is only one outcome as you finally have your last shred of critical thought process taken away and exit for the team lobotomy. Your other choice is to drop out and go to a different school. The problem is there are a lot of similar high schools out there, creating the dilemma of where do you go next?

The high school group also still likes toys. They are just a little more sophisticated in their approach. For example, someone decides it's cool to have an Enterprise Customer Relationship Software "Solution," or completely re-architect their technology infrastructure. Now, since they have some education, they know that toy acquisitions must be dressed up in some sort of "rational" business case, such as improving processing efficiency, enabling future growth through technology refresh, or enhancing the customers' buying experience. But it is just another toy. If you don't already communicate with your customers, purchasing a "relationship" software program won't help. Of course, that wasn't the point to begin with since you were just fooling yourself or maybe just the boss. If you did believe this would fix your problem of poor processes and dysfunctional team members you may just be unfit for duty in your current position.

High School is harder to fix than Grade School because your "problems" are educated enough to modify their behavior on a moment's notice. Just like a member of a high school clique they can act like a real jerk to their team and when they sit with their boss, or more importantly the HR director or CEO, transform into a completely different personality. These are your team chameleons; evil creatures that thrive in the high school team environment. Depending on your level in the organization they can completely change their personality. This includes emotional instability at times, just like grade school. Who doesn't love a team leader who throws temper tantrums and changes direction at a moment's notice or explanation. You also see fighting over inconsequential matters, such as what office furniture each level in the school clique should possess. It is still definitely all about me although there is at least an awareness of a larger world. There are some people on the team who are serious. Their goal is to just put in their time long enough to graduate, i.e., quit and get a real job at an adult company.

There are teams that demonstrate some of the characteristics of a high school team, with the capability of occasionally functioning at a slightly higher maturity level. In some areas of your school the level borders on adult behavior. You may still have the various cliques, but with more cross-functional socializing and efforts made to make projects successful. This happens because everyone is at least nominally aware that the teams must work together to get something done. This level can be harder or easier to change depending on the situation. Easier because mature individuals and teams understand the importance of good operations and achieving financial goals to keep the business going and their paychecks intact. Harder because things may be working well enough and team leaders will display passive-aggressive behavior. This includes agreeing that things need to change and then throwing up subtle roadblocks to any changes required. This is also the group that is more likely to try team builders where everyone declares success. Of course, you really don't see any major improvement in projects or outcomes, but you can check off the box and tell the CEO how successful the program was.

Adult Education: Autodidacts (Self-learners)

First of all, I am excited to finally be able to use one of my favorite words, autodidact, in a sentence. Secondly it signifies something you need to look for in every employee—being a self-learner. You will rarely hear 'someone needs to give me training' among autodidacts. Give them the opportunity and they will do it themselves. They understand and support the metrics in place. There is also an understanding that the success of the company has a direct impact on their success both personally and financially. They work on teams when appropriate and ensure their teams are staffed with the correct individuals for the tasks required for success. Truly empowered by management there is less organizational resistance since everyone on the team is aligned to the high-level success criteria of the company. In other words, a team every leader says they want but few ever create. There are two main reasons for this:

- Most leaders don't really want this type of team.
- It is hard work.

Many team leaders who claim they want this type of team really don't. As discussed in Chapter 3 on human nature, these leaders typically rise to these positions because they want prestige, power over others, and more money. Competence is confused with position within the hierarchy and the ability to spin any problem to deflect responsibility.

For those leaders who really want this type of team it is the hardest organizational model to sustain because it is a dynamic one. People change, products change, and the environment around the team changes. Adult teams require constant honest analysis, communication, and engagement from all levels to keep the teams on track. In other words, there are not very many of these teams around. The good news is there is a subset within many organizations that do maintain this structure. For example, even if your sales area is in grade school, the product area is being run as an adult center and can manage sales with risk mitigation strategies.

Having worked on products as well as having been on and worked with sales teams, I have an idea how much patience is required for this to work. If you need help in this area, I recommend using a singing bowl and meditating. The adult team continues to look for ways to work with the various teams or find alternative resources and ask forgiveness later. The important thing is they are successful and have the metrics to prove it. The adult teams never surrender to the non-performers or the immature. They come up with plans to attempt risk mitigation for the team and work towards the overall organizational success. I didn't say it will always work, just that it sometimes works. At some point it is possible for some executives to start seeing a measurable gap between the producers and the non-producers and the light starts to be directed on the few teams left that still don't get it. Remember, I just said it was possible. It is also possible as an adult that you will give up and just take your singing bowl and meditation skills to a new team.

I have seen this on a firsthand basis with an adult manager who reported to a director at the grade school level who reported to a grade school/high school executive who reported to a High School Chief. The technical term for what this manager had to do to be effective in this organizational nightmare is called living in management team hell. There was no support from senior management, which required the person to navigate this dysfunctional team. This leader still set goals, insisted on quality work from her people, and the team was successful. She didn't give up and lower her commitment to excellence due to the antics of her boss and her CLO, Chief Loser Officer.

Unfortunately for the team, as any mature adult would do when the right opportunity presented itself, she was ready to move on and leave this situation behind. Within two years after her self-graduation to an adult team the kindergarten cops running the place had ruined the department and its reputation with both customers and the executives. The only silver lining was it helped exposed the incompetency of a grade school team leader who was finally shown the door. The only reason it happened was the grade school ringleader became a liability to the high school clique leader. Of course, this decision wasn't made until after there was long-term damage to the overall team.

Once you have achieved an adult organization the biggest risk becomes monitoring the gate regarding whom you let in. One grade school member in a position of authority on a team can do severe damage if not stopped in time. If you have an executive who ignores an issue with a direct report because the team reporting to her is keeping the machine running, you are playing a risky game. At some point you will lose great individuals just because you can't decide to remove someone from a level that they are not qualified to be at.

WHERE ARE YOU?

Where are you, your company, division, and work team in terms of maturity? The good news is once you have identified the level you can make the move to adult supervision. It your team is in grade school you don't have to move them to high school first. Skip it and go directly to adult education. Some people will never get to adult supervision or want to go there. You must expel them from school and let them ruin another organization with their idea of teaming— more on that in the next chapters.

As we also discuss in the next chapters, assessing where individuals are will show where the team is. It is critical to understand that one 'team' member may ruin the performance of an entire team. Ignoring the situation will not make it go away. Your mission is to start to see what maturity level each team member is at and determine how to address the situation. This is an area where you don't have to be dependent on your executive team making a decision. You can start making an assessment today where you and your team are and what the plan is going to be to make the change. Make the plan, coach those who are willing to engage, and expel those who will not.

It's a simple formula that many team leaders find difficult to execute. Again, there is only one cure for grade school and high school mentality: the FOM treatment. No matter how much a grade school or high school leader charms you, they will soon be gone after you have called their bluff. The good news is these outwardly looking dynamic team members will probably move on to your competitors, joining their high school musical cast, all for your long-term benefit.

CHAPTER 9

THE FIRST STEP: COMMITMENT TO CHANGE

"We can't solve problems by using the same kind of thinking we used when we created them."

ALBERT EINSTEIN

You have identified where the team, your work group, and individuals on the team are in terms of maturity. There is one thing left before embarking on your journey. What about you? Before you change your team, you must change yourself. Your outlook, your approach, and your definition of success should be realigned to the goal of creating a high-performance team. You can change leaders, change processes, change every aspect of your team. If you don't commit to real change for yourself, it will not matter. The main reason teams fail is a lack of commitment to team success. Of course, this is the last thing any team leader would admit to. Instead, there is always an excuse. We didn't communicate enough. We didn't fund the project enough, contracted with the wrong vendors, or other departments are a bottleneck, etc., etc., etc.

TEAMWORK MOMENT OF TRUTH

Everyone is committed to the word teamwork. Few will do the work for the team.

Today there appears to be a strong commitment to the word teamwork—not actual teamwork. The actions of everyone from the leadership level on down sends the opposite message. Another way to tell there is a lack of commitment to teamwork is to see how many "Teamwork" signs are in a department. Every time I hear someone say we need to work as a team it tells me they don't EVER work as a team. It also tells me that the person defines teamwork as everyone working to meet their individual needs. Ask yourself how many times you say we need to work as a team when you meant help me with my objective. We pretend we need teamwork to achieve the mission and goal of the organization when we just mean drop what you're doing and take care of my needs. This may come as a surprise, but the team does not think taking care of your needs is the goal of teamwork. Attempting to just suppress individual goals in support of some universal team goal is the work of insane people with no insight into human nature. If individual goals are not aligned to the team goal, why in the world would anyone think a team will work?

TEAMWORK MOMENT OF TRUTH

Teamwork is inversely proportional to the number of times everyone says teamwork is important.

What is the first step in your journey? Recognizing the need to change and commit to it. A leader must truly commit to change. Not just say it but do it. That doesn't mean printing up posters, buying cards to memorize, or adding "Change is a way of life" mottos on your web site. You must have the vision, commit to it, and start to devise the strategies to get you there. Once you have the strategies and metrics in place you must work to achieve results. If your team is not performing and you have not done anything to improve the situation, including the hard decision of replacing non-performers on the team, you are still not committed. Save yourself some cost, quit training teams, hiring consultants, and initiating eight fat sigma methodologies, or hiring a team coach. It is a waste of your time and the team's money. You can then show an immediate positive increase in your bottom line by just eliminating all this costly activity that produces nothing.

TEAMWORK MOMENT OF TRUTH

"Most people know what needs to be done. They just don't do what needs to be done.

You have the potential to set in motion a series of cultural changes overnight which are so powerful you will be amazed at the progress your team will make as it gathers momentum. Are you truly ready to commit to real goals and objectives? Your sincere commitment to change will come through in every interaction with your employees and other departments. Your credibility will grow as you demonstrate you are following through on your commitments to build and execute your improvement plan. All the plans, all the strategies, all the changes will not matter without the individual commitment to try. If you have convinced yourself that it is a team problem and not about the individuals on your team, then your long-term problems will not be solved.

Wow that was easy! Absolutely not! The first thing you must change is how you view organizations and what it means to be a team leader. You must fight powerful forces in society that are moving away from an emphasis on individual achievement and more toward some nebulous love of the team concept. This view is infiltrating everything from government to business to youth sports. There is always a focus on how to make a team accountable without any critical thought as to what an excellent team consists of. A team is a group of individuals who are driven to achieve or not to achieve. By driven I don't mean by whips and guns to their heads, but by their choice.

COMMITMENT TO A POSITIVE OUTLOOK

If the old saying that eighty percent of success is just showing up, then the next fifteen percent can be reached with a commitment to excellence backed with a positive outlook. Dedicating yourself to be the best you can be will change the course of your life. There will always be negative group energy that impacts an individual wanting to achieve more in life. Eliminating this roadblock to individual success is very difficult. When I was a field engineer at one location "the team" would get together for lunch at a local restaurant every day. Every day I would show up and hear nothing but complaints about the job, the boss, the customers, and life in general. No conversations on how to improve processes, client relationships, or themselves. If only the world would get in line and change everything would be great. Here is an obvious news flash. The world will never get in line because the world is not that into you. If the world decided to get in line, you wouldn't like that either, given your current attitude.

I began to recognize that having lunch with this group was having a negative impact on my outlook, my approach to my job, and achievement of my personal goals. Groupthink is a powerful force that can destroy the efforts of any team. In my late twenties I didn't understand on a conscious level what was going on. I did finally realize that I had to remove myself from this group and eat lunch either by myself or associate myself with people who had a more positive outlook as opposed to this toxic, ongoing negativity. Many people don't realize this trap their entire lives and continue on the same path until the end.

You will find this in whatever job situation you are in. When you attempt to change, don't expect the team to be very supportive. No matter what level you are on it is likely that you will be viewed as a threat to others. You will be a threat because on some level others do not want to face the real reasons they are unhappy and the fact that doing something different is possible but requires them to act. Others will be afraid that a lifetime of positioning themselves with the boss and staying out of trouble may not be enough if you are successful. Therefore, attempts will be made to sabotage everything you are trying to do for yourself and your team. You must have the internal compass that tells you this is the right thing to do regardless of what others may say, think, or attempt to do.

This doesn't mean you adopt a Pollyanna world view. There are real problems that occur which can damage attitudes of individuals and will impact your team. For example, you may be joining a team that just went through a major downsizing. People are bitter and have seen their friends who "worked hard" let go. It won't matter whether the layoff was fair. It will matter what happens after the lay-offs. Those who are committed and dedicated will provide value and excellence. Those who have always done the minimum will continue to get the minimum from their life. There are many examples you can point to of people who appear to lead a charmed life, doing little yet reaping big rewards. Yes, it sucks that somebody else won the lottery. The point is it doesn't matter. You must concern yourself with your future. This raises the odds for not only a successful work career but a life you can look back on with satisfaction. If you are in an orga-nization that doesn't appreciate this outlook, use your time there to increase your skills, provide them with the best work possible, and the look for your next opportunity elsewhere. Be a realist. Some sit-uations you won't be able to change.

You hear sports analogies constantly about how a team never wins without the commitment by every individual to achieve the success of the team no matter what the personal sacrifice. As someone who has had the pleasure to coach sports teams, I can tell you there is a big difference between players on teams where the players want to be there and play, and those whose mommy and daddy are making them play. Some may have all the talent in the world but are not motivated to do a good job. They see no joy or benefit in it for them. Others squeeze out every last bit of talent they have in order to achieve the objective. They know they can't score as many goals, be a goal ten-der, or be the best defender in the league, but they work hard and master their position. Using 100% of the talent they do have and playing consistently moves them far ahead of many more allegedly "talented" individuals. These are the people who will make you com-petitive and potentially bring you the win over a team that appears on paper to be stronger and more talented.

There is a reason teams are easier to manage when they are winning. They are winning because the individuals are talented AND using that talent to the best of their ability to achieve clear, outlined goals. The only time managing a winning team is harder is when management has confused winning with coddling perceived "experts" as if they can't be replaced. Once the team sees different rules being applied to different people then organizational structure starts to break down. Sometimes you are much better off trading the .400 hitter who creates problems in the clubhouse and on the field for a player who is motivated—and also has the talent—to succeed. You may need to ship out your one so-called expert who refuses to be governed by all your metrics.

See the correlation? You have people on your team who don't want to be there. They do not care for the team, and only because you have not motivated them to quit are they still playing. In many cases it is because they don't even have enough ambition to help themselves and get a job they would like to do. Oh, there is no one on your team that thinks that? OK, sure thing. Just keep believing those employee survey scores where all your employees tell you how super "engaged" they are, and your company is truly the best place in the world to work.

TEAMWORK MOMENT OF TRUTH

You must commit to helping poor performing team members find what they love to do by removing them from the team you need to build.

You must also commit to have the individuals on your team attempt to be the best they can be at their work. You must commit to try no matter what level in the organization you find yourself in. This is not done by cheerleading or paying lip service to the boss. It means a commitment to create and meet the realistic goals and objectives for the team. You as the team leader must commit to support the team in any way you can. Once they have bought in to the metrics and trust your system it is up to you to continually earn that trust by consistently following the rules of metrics and accountability for your team and yourself. Finally, you must commit to help the team by removing team members who can't or won't achieve the individual metrics required by the team to be successful.

The most powerful resistance you will receive is the power of negative thinking. Everywhere people turn they are bombarded by the negative messages in society. You can't get ahead. People are hurting. The rich get richer. Layoffs, pestilence, plague. The news media and social media commentators thrive on negative images and appear dedicated to making people as miserable as possible. Politicians tell us how bad everything is, and our only hope is to elect them, as if that ever works. Even the ones who have been in office twenty years continue to run on the same message that they are all the stands between you and impending doom.

Unfortunately, there are a lot of incentives for them to do this: getting your vote, subscribing to their feed, reading their articles, or reaping monetary rewards. Based on the number of politicians who become multimillionaires after being elected to help the common folk and take money away from rich people, you can make a case that getting you to vote for them has large personal monetary incentives for them. Before you claim I just violated my own positive cynical approach to people by broad brushing politicians, let me clarify. If someone new is elected I will first be positive that they may truly be different and attempt to follow through on their promises. However, based on the number of politicians who have significantly expanded their net worth by millions of dollars while claiming to be for "the underdog," I will remain cynical they will follow through with their promises unless they deliver with results.

To counteract negativity, team leaders usually attempt to generate more positive messages. Unfortunately, the message generally focuses on mindless cheerleading and slogans about how great the team is. Then leaders order people to be more positive, which is always a great way to help the team achieve more. After this fails a "strategy" is created to tell team members they have a negative attitude and need to change if they want to achieve greatness. These types of "action plans" are not a solution and only insults your team's intelligence.

Don't be a cheerleader with advertising slogans. That is not leadership. Your team will sniff out your insincerity in about 3.2 seconds, crushing your credibility. Focus on the positive without ignoring the reality of the negative. Leading by example with the positive benefits of meeting the metrics as a focal point will help employees who have lost their desire to succeed due to all the negative forces around them at work and in their personal life. These negative influences have brought them to the point of believing there is no point in excellence, creativity, and hard work. Only by looking past this negativity can you focus on positive improvement. If you dedicate yourself to excellence and expect more from others you will get more. People feed on genuine enthusiasm and positive direction. The opposite happens when you are phony and your actions are contrary to your words.

Now you have the commitment and the fire in your belly to take the hill. But wait a minute; you may be forgetting a couple of items. Like a person who converts to a new religion you are excited to tell everyone about it. After all, once they hear it they will be just as excited as you are! Well, before you dress up in robes and shout out 'I have Changed" and hand out the "Book of Holy Positive Changes" to your employees while you dance in front of the building, stop and consider what this will mean to your employees. Besides concern for your mental stability they will express over the toga you are wearing and your chants in the parking lot, there are other things to consider. such as this Teamwork Moment of Truth.

TEAMWORK MOMENT OF TRUTH

Nothing is easier than telling the Team they need to change. Nothing is harder than leading a Team to change, starting with you.

RECOGNIZE HOW HARD CHANGE IS

I can't emphasize enough how important this is no matter what level you are at. Do not underestimate the powerful forces at work in every organization and teams that put up roadblocks. Did I say roadblocks? They are figuratively building their own personal Le Mont-Saint-Michel. This Abbey is located on the coast of Normandy. You can walk to the entrance of the fortifications and attempt to enter only during low tide. At times of high tide it is surrounded by water. Even during the Hundred Years' Warr between France and England during the Middle Ages, the Abbey was never conquered. This is the type of defense that will be planned and built against you and your silly team improvement plans.

LE MONT-SAINT-MICHEL

Now that you are on board there are only a couple of other problems you must overcome. If you recall from Chapter Two, we called them the Roadblocks to Success. I can speak with you and have you all fired up and ready to go, and ride into the sunset. Two weeks later you are feeling drained and depressed. Why? The negativity that is all around you starts to work its ugly magic. These negative forces will get you down on occasion no matter how much positive energy you have.

As mentioned earlier, one coping mechanism I found helpful throughout my career that you might need to employ is the Cynical Positive Approach to overcome the roadblocks in your mind. The Cynical Positive Approach recognizes that a positive attitude and approach are the keys to success in everything you attempt in life. While they are the key to success in your life, never expect everyone or for that matter anyone else to jump on board with your program. If they do, be pleasantly surprised. It should not change your approach.

A Pollyanna positive approach is delusional at best and fake cheerleading at worse. You must rely upon your own character and what is right. Others will follow because you will be among the few who lead in a positive manner. You will gain respect by earning it. When you communicate with those who don't appear to have a positive outlook, don't ask if they are ready to have a positive attitude. If they have signed on to the metrics and accountability, don't ask them to fake it with cheerleading and demand they have the same personality, approach, and attitude as you. The best you will get is fake conformity to a positive outlook. Remember you will take a few steps back on occasion. No matter how positive I have been about the future there were and still are times I throw up my hands and succumb to negative thoughts and behaviors. It's what you do to address those inevitable moments to get you back on track that is important.

Why do you need a Cynical Positive mindset? Powerful roadblocks don't move just because you decide to go down a different path. If anything, they will initially take it up another notch, thinking that your "new" idea is a fad that can be dosed with a hose full of cold, relentless obstruction. If you win the fight for yourself then you can proceed to take on in a positive manner all the various people who are standing in the way of success.

The only one you have now eliminated from the list of team issues is you. The good news is that was the biggest roadblock of all. Your commitment is the most effective weapon to address all the other roadblocks to success and overcome them. Recognize what to change. This is why it is important to perform an analysis of the current state of the team, the maturity level, and appropriate metrics before making decisions on team execution. While the decision on team execution may be an actual team execution, there may be a faster way to achieve the goals required for success.

TEAMWORK MOMENT OF TRUTH

Sometimes the team doesn't need to change; you need to change something for the team.

The first thing that must change is you and your approach to managing teams. You must undo years of bad habits and communication problems. You must be ready to become more accountable to your team and the metrics as well as ask team members to become accountable. If, as a leader, you provide challenging and rewarding work along with accountability and authority, you will attract talent at all levels. You can't just say it, or put up posters saying it, or make it a company strategy. You must live it.

All of this on some level appears to be common sense. The challenge is knowing what to do intellectually gets lost in the day-to-day activities of your work and coping with the antics of the various teams you are interacting with. You may know it, but what have you really been doing for your team lately to help them be better? What have you been doing for yourself lately to make you better? Sometimes giving the right metrics and direction is all that it takes to turn a team from low to high performance. I have taken over the management of allegedly unsalvageable teams. Sometimes, since there is such a high degree of dysfunctional thinking in a team, there is a tendency to want to eliminate everything. The easiest path can appear to be to disband the team. The problem with this approach is without solving the root cause the new team will quickly devolve into the same behavior over time. You may as well put the metrics in place and see if the team in place can perform first. Again, focus on the financial and operational metrics, demand accountability, and then replace team members who are incapable of change.

This is why it's important to perform the proper, honest analysis. What are the things that are working in this organization? Why are they working? Why are they not working? Maybe the right metrics are in place, but no one felt it was important to measure the results. In one case I knew some members of the team were lazy or even lacked the ability to perform their jobs. I had to force myself to recognize that some people had been operating for years under metrics that were bad or non-existent. I owed it to the team members to say here is what you will be measured on going forward and then give them the support and opportunity to be successful. Many responded to the challenge. Some did not.

It all comes down to the individual. How does a person overcome a lifetime of disappointment and failed attempts at achievement? How do they find the place within themselves that enables them to focus on positive achievement and make a change in their work environment? Just because the epiphany came to you doesn't mean all you have to do is show people the way. Many will refuse to believe and battle you all the way. You must prepare yourself for this battle.

In the next chapter, we'll discuss how to prepare your battle plan for tackling the many difficult roadblocks—namely, people—that stand in the way of team success. Some of the team will not make it. Others will surprise you as they see your example and it lights something within them that they never knew they had. Your commitment to leading by example is what works. Not the team posters, the speeches, or the assurances. Now get ready because you have some work cut out for you in the next chapter. You will need every positive coping mechanism you have as you continue your journey to a high-performing team.

CHAPTER 10

OVERCOMING THE CULTURE THROUGH METRICS

*"You have set yourselves a difficult task,
but you will succeed if you persevere; and
you will find joy in overcoming obstacles."*

HELEN KELLER

D o not underestimate the culture of any team and your ability
to change it in a short period of time. As an executive, manager, or individual contributor you must also realize that consciously,
or unconsciously, you are responsible for the culture of your team
over the long term. Just because you read this book and realized you
are part of the problem doesn't mean you can change it by executive edict. If you at least recognize that a culture change is necessary for your team to survive, then congratulations, you are on
your way to victory. Of course, this would be victory as defined by
a cynical optimist, meaning the potential exists of this being a pyr-
rhic victory for you.

> **TEAMWORK MOMENT OF TRUTH**
>
> The only way to change the culture is to change what you measure.

Stop right now. Do not call a Culture Consultant or Team Coach. This will buy you some amazing colorful slides full of buzz words, feel-good pabulum, some complicated graphs and statistics on employee engagement, constant surveys, and other tasks that will do nothing to solve the problem. This is not completely true. The team will finally start filling out the employee surveys telling you how happy they are just to avoid filling out any more surveys, fake action plans, or pretend how much this program is making a difference. Ask yourself; are you a leader or not? As a leader you must recognize the only way to change the culture is to change how you are measuring your team members and then hold everyone accountable to that standard. This includes your nephew, who is such a dynamic personality and at least appears very loyal to the company. No results to show? Then he must go! Culture change is hard.

There are certain steps you should follow no matter if you are the long-term leader of a team or the new leader of a team you have never managed before. For you team management veterans, if you follow the same steps as if you just received the assignment, you can force yourself to look more objectively at the current situation. Even if you are partly, or more likely, completely responsible for how the department was staffed, as well as behaves. Since you have made the commitment to change you must start at the beginning.

STEP 1: DO NOTHING

The first step is what NOT to do. And that starts with standing up and announcing a big change is happening—effective immediately. Congratulations, you have just made your job twice as hard. The sergeants, who were here long before you, will rally their platoons for resistance. After all you are but one of a series of "leaders" who said change was coming, typically followed by the usual pabulum that "change is good, and we must change to be successful." Even if the team wants change, and that is a big IF, why should they trust you? The last five "change events" were failures and they have the coffee mugs at home to prove it. In fact, they shouldn't trust you and you shouldn't expect them to. If they have built their own metrics about what is great performance due to a lack of any direction from the last manager or organization they were in, you will immediately be seen as a threat. What if you give them stupid metrics that have nothing to do with the function of the team? What if your metrics make them less valuable? Even if you hear nothing but acceptance and support, a year later absolutely nothing will have changed as far as results. When coming into a new organization or starting change in your own organization the first thing to do is NOTHING!

What makes this advice difficult to implement is that one of the definitions of a leader is to act, and I just told you not to take any action. Why? Because you have no idea what the hell is going on no matter what your boss, vice president, CEO, or the Chairman of the Board told you. Refer to any number of references in this book on typical leadership in organizations if you think they know. You may "know" that everyone thinks your division, department, or team must improve, but why? Lost money, client satisfaction scores are bad, your employees are hard to work with, excessive complaints about product quality, or projects are never completed successfully. At this point you don't know and are just guessing. As excited as you are about announcing your new, big-brain idea methodology effective tomorrow, take a deep breath and proceed with the following step.

STEP 2: RESEARCH THE SITUATION

Meet with employees individually from various areas. Ask them the following questions:

1. What do you think your job is?

2. What is your team's function? What part does your department play in the success of the company?

3. What do you like and dislike about the organization?

4. Who in their group or department do they look to for leadership?

5. What does the department do well?

6. What areas need improvement?

7. What are the first three things you would like to see changed?

TEAMWORK MOMENT OF TRUTH

There will be no shortage of people on the team who will tell you everything is great. Those people are lying.

Yes, some people will tell you nothing at all and others will say that everything is great and there are no problems. These people are, of course, lying. Others will act like they speak for everyone on the team. They are typically delusional. Don't argue no matter how incredibly stupid the answers are, and yes, some of the ideas will be incredibly stupid. Have you ever heard the expression that there is no such thing as a stupid idea? Well, yes, there are stupid ideas— lots of them. The most stupid idea of all is the idea that there are no stupid ideas. Even if you agree with an employee, don't go out of your way to agree with them. The key thing is to shut up and listen. While you listen take notes. Taking notes demonstrates you are making a record of what they say and are taking it seriously, even the stupid ideas. The reason you must take the stupid ideas seriously is they are a window into that employee's world view. That view may be shaped by their supervisor, previous boss, some company training, or a serious psychotic condition that you need to be concerned about. Nevertheless, it is important in your analysis.

Some will be testing you with answers they think you want to hear. Be careful to nod and take notes but not pontificate because you are grateful to have found at least one ally in your quest to improve the team. The person could be the exact opposite, someone who tries to endear themselves to the boss to avoid accountability, or worse, is just trying to gather intelligence on what you think. After gathering the additional intel, they can report back to the platoon leaders to assist in developing battle strategies to resist. Finally, you will get some great perspectives from the great individual contributors, which will open your eyes to additional possibilities and ways to overcome challenges. You goal is to have more of these team members at the end of the process than when you started.

While you are collecting this information you are also discovering the general culture of the team. Is there a certain amount of groupthink in their world view? Does everyone give you the same "speech" as if it were memorized before they met with you? Has the group developed a victim syndrome? No one understands us. If only everyone else would do their job, we would be successful. Warning: depending on how bad the situation is you may find yourself ready to jump off a bridge or just fire every last whining baby who has "needs." Resist the temptation and be patient. I have seen many individual contributors turn around their performance when finally given some logical direction from an effective leader. Remember to hold your fire, as there are a few steps left. Keep in mind I didn't say you should not eventually fire some people or have them pursue other interests. Just hold off until you have a comprehensive plan in place to give good people the chance to succeed.

The next step is to talk to the people outside your department who work with your team. What is their perception? What is the customers' perception of your products and services? You don't need a consultant. If the company is allegedly paying you for your leadership skills, now is the time to employ them. Ask people yourself. This serves two purposes. You are gathering information firsthand so you can make quality decisions and you are also building valuable relationships for future interactions with people outside the team. Who are the customers of your department? Ask them. What are they looking for? What do they like and dislike? Just like your employees you will get some amazing answers. Remember, many times other teams are still in the "do things for me only" mode and could care less about process improvements in their own areas. Even the most dysfunctional areas can have insights that you will be able to use in your analysis.

You will also find valuable information about areas that will need risk mitigation strategies because they are in one of the lower maturity grades. The reason you need risk strategies is that some other "teams" won't ever be interested in improvement. They will only look at you as a threat because you are successful and that may hamper their efforts in securing promotions or other self-serving activities. You will need risk mitigation strategies to neutralize these teams and their efforts at sabotaging your team. If something is out of your control don't waste precious time attempting to fix it. You have enough to do.

What does the boss think? Your boss's boss? How does your team fit into the strategic objectives of your department/division/company? Remember, the boss is only one perspective. They typically just want a problem fixed or their operation to run well. Your job is root cause analysis and making problems go away, the right way, long term. This advice is much easier said than done because this group of "stakeholders" is directly responsible for signing your paychecks. This is an important consideration when you are determining which stakeholder opinion matters more in the short term. Unfortunately, many people in team leadership roles only take the boss perspective into consideration. This is bad short-term thinking for you and your long-term success. The key is to weave their requirements into your individual metrics without sacrificing what you are trying to achieve long term. If you try to just fix the boss issue of the week it will be like hitting the gopher heads with a mallet at an arcade game. Every day more gophers will pop up as you spend your time "fixing" the latest crisis. Meanwhile, you are fixing nothing long term and may be sacrificed by the boss if she is in trouble with her boss due to gopher fatigue syndrome.

TEAMWORK MOMENT OF TRUTH

Hitting gopher heads can be fun and gives the illusion of progress—until the boss decides you and the team are gophers too.

Fixing the root cause issue instead of attacking the crisis de jour sounds like a fundamental managerial tactic that everyone should "know." They don't, don't remember, or it has never mattered in any team management job they've held in the past. If you never use the concepts, it won't be long before they fall into disuse. Another reason the fundamentals of team problem solving are not considered is that typically a new leader is immediately thrown into day-to-day issues of an operation that needs to be fixed now. Analysis and planning are immediately put on the back burner as they move into survival mode. Even if everyone is in grade school, you must rise above this even if it means short-term pain for yourself, e.g., investing significant time outside of "normal" business hours or getting advice from a grade school boss.

The most significant reason the analysis steps are given lip service is not only are you action oriented, but your boss typically is also. She wants results NOW! Her job may be on the line if she doesn't show she is fixing something. I suggest giving her a large PowerPoint of at least 120 slides with color graphs and animation. Throw in multiple business buzzwords. Yes, even use the evil word Synergy if your boss is semi-delusional. Whatever it takes to buy some time. Remember that you can do this analysis in a relatively short period of time even for large teams. It needs to be thorough and honest, and you have some hard work in front of you. Concurrently, always be on the lookout for the evil twin brother of not doing appropriate analysis before action—analysis paralysis. There are people who, if given the opportunity, will perform analysis forever to avoid making any hard decisions. If you have those types of "leaders" on your team it may be time for a change in that area as well.

STEP 3: DEFINE THE METRICS

Now it's time to work on all those operational and financial metrics we talked about in the previous chapters. Forget about who is on your current team and whether they have the ability to do what needs to be done. First, what are the financial and operational metrics your team needs to be successful? Everything we have previously discussed about metrics needs to be considered specific to your team at this point. You have all your research data available. Now use it. If the overall metrics have been articulated well at an overall team level, you will have an easier time defining them for your team. If, I mean when, you discover that metrics are not all that well-thought-out at any level above your team on the organizational chart, the real fun begins. You get to guess. The good news is that even if the metrics are fuzzy above you, it doesn't excuse you from creating metrics that are clear at your level. Use industry best practices, your background, discussions with team leaders you report to. From this you have an excellent starting point to put metrics in place.

After putting your metrics together get your boss to commit to your metrics. Explain the metrics to your boss and how they will improve the performance of your team and help her achieve her goals. Make sure your metrics address her pain points. This serves two purposes:

1. Boss buy-in helps when the allegedly "critical employee" in your boss's mind goes over your head to complain about the negative impact of your new changes. More on that later.

2. If your boss is still in grade school or high school but agrees to let you go forward, they are less likely to become a roadblock later, or if they become a roadblock can be managed appropriately. Notice I said less likely.

You can pontificate all day about how you need to add quality to the assembly line. If you boss's pain point is sales complaining about quality, you should understand what sales believes is the quality problem. Then ensure it is captured as part of your action plan to address her pain point. Addressing quality should stop the complaints from the boss unless the boss thinks quality is defined as the big boss doesn't complain about something even if it is unrelated to anything pertaining to a metric. This is a highly understated, illogical, and sometimes uber stupid metric, yet an important metric to consider how to address.

Now you need to take the overall team metrics and match them to individual roles on the team. What are the individual performance metrics that will enable the team to achieve the overall goal? How does their job support the team's financial and operational goals? If you are having a difficult time defining it, maybe that job isn't as necessary as you thought. Beware of the individual goals that sound important yet when you peel back and look under the covers you find nothing there. One example is someone responsible for driving a ten percent productivity gain across all teams. Who defines productivity? Is the person really driving productivity or just gathering data and putting it on an awesome presentation slide with animation? The vaguer the metrics for a position the more likely these are jobs that were given to people who were not effective in their last position. Especially on larger teams, it is sometimes easier to relegate people to jobs with great titles and hope they don't do any long-term damage to the overall organization.

People in management positions who want to demonstrate to the boss, customers, or their board they are "doing something" about an issue also tend to hire a methodology "expert" in quality, process, communications, or whatever they have been told is a "problem." If you have team members with titles such as Innovation Manager, Vice President of Operational Efficiency, Director Organizational Productivity, Vice President of Client Satisfaction, or Chief Vision Officer, these are symptoms of a team in trouble.

There are two explanations for having team members such as those:

1. Someone realized there was a problem with efficiency, productivity, or satisfaction and couldn't figure out how to make the teams responsible to improve them.

2. Someone is collecting a welfare check from the "team." This could be for a myriad of reasons, including an executive likes them, they are friends with someone "high up," or any number of excuses that add cost and hurt the long-term viability of the organization.

The previous explanations don't necessarily apply to your organization. I am sure your SVP of Employee Happiness is doing a great job for you.

TEAMWORK MOMENT OF TRUTH

Creating individual metrics that are definable and measurable is easy. Defining relevant metrics that improve
team performance is hard.

If you want to avoid adding these types of cost, you must do more
work defining metrics. There are many teams that define and measure
metrics. Are you sure the metrics are relevant? Beware of the stupid
metric discussed in Chapter 6! If you create a metric such as developing ten new products this year and compensate the team for success,
I guarantee your team will create ten new products. I didn't say they
would be good products, or relevant, profitable, or even real products. By the time the executive presentation is delivered on measuring success I guarantee there will be ten bullets with product names
after them because that's what you told the boss was going to happen.
If you stepped back and think this through, you will start to see how
ridiculous some of the metrics are. Unfortunately for the long-term
health of the team, in our attempt to come up with something measurable we succumb to the temptation of calling a tactic to achieve a
goal an actual goal.

Now that you have the metrics established, what do you think
happens on many teams at this point? Amazingly, nothing! There are
vague references at meetings and possibly a general understanding.
If you ask the people on the team, don't be surprised how different
everyone thinks the obvious success metrics are.

STEP 4: PUBLISH THE METRICS

You now have the metrics and have three options on what to do with them:

1. Forget about them. After all we have another crisis to manage this week.

2. Save them to a folder and refer to them when you write the employee annual performance appraisal

3. Publish them and refer to them consistently throughout the year

No one admits they do option one, yet that is the typical approach in most organizations that even bother to articulate the metrics. If they are doing metrics at all they are fuzzy team metrics. The opposite end of the spectrum involves the individual metrics not associated with the overall team goals. Once people achieve the wrong goal people say, "Aha, see we told you that focusing on the individual gets the wrong results." As discussed in previous chapters, since you did not take the time to truly define the appropriate individual metrics to support the team, the department, the division, and the company, you got excellent individual results that hurt the overall team efforts. Remember our discussion on good financial and quality metrics to ensure you are providing the appropriate individual goals.

The Team Member Performance Appraisal

While the first order of business is to publish the metrics that will be utilized to measure performance, nothing brings the point home faster than publishing an individual performance appraisal template currently used by your organization and that will be used to rate and determine the type of raise the individual receives. Publish how the goals will fit into the general performance appraisal form six months to a year ahead of the appraisal process. Discussing this with each team member focuses attention on the direct benefits of meeting the operational and financial objectives and shows this is how we will measure success over the year. This tends to work slightly better than basing your super-secret annual performance review on whatever the employee did last week that you happened to remember.

With everything that has been written about performance appraisals, at this point you would think telling people in advance what the metrics are, how this translates into their individual appraisal and raise, and then following though, would be universally used across all teams. As with everything else we have discussed, with the current "leadership" in place for many teams, theory and reality are two very separate ideas. I didn't claim every team doesn't have a great appraisal methodology. Of course, every HR department in high school and some grade school teams use a form and have documented the appraisal process. The issue is, what you are documenting, how are you applying the process, and what do you follow through on?

TEAMWORK MOMENT OF TRUTH

Stop focusing on the tools and start focusing on the content.

There are at least 500 performance appraisal tools you can research to use. There are also 500 claw hammers in the marketplace you can buy. Any tool can be used. Please just pick one and focus on content and what the end goal is.

STEP 5: MEASURE AGAINST THE METRICS

Some team members will not be happy with measuring for a variety of reasons, such as:

- They are used to having the image of being one of the best at what they do. The problem was they got to define what "best" is. Now that you are defining best as the voice of the client they might not look as good. This is a difficult thing for an employee to deal with if they have been coddled for years

- Many people fall into the trap of not wanting to be accountable. They want to be rewarded but don't want accountability. If you take over a department that is dysfunctional or has had no metrics, chances are people with this attitude gravitated to that department and stayed there for obvious reasons. Now you are changing their world.

If you've published the metrics on the standard performance appraisal form your team uses, you are already halfway home. They know the metrics, they understand the results that you want, and they can see the results. Measuring against the metrics on performance appraisals has such a bad name because most leaders do not create an appraisal that attempts to measure against any real metrics. A "good" performance rating on an appraisal may say you do an excellent job with customer service, but there is no metric as to why the team leader reached that conclusion. Are you going to argue with the good rating? Do you ask the leader how in the world she came up with a high rating in a certain category?

After thirty years of being subjected to, witnessing, and hearing hundreds of performance appraisal horror stories, it is safe to say it is the norm across all teams and organizations. We all have stories like these because most team leaders do not get their jobs by having the skills to be effective team managers. Refer to the previous chapters on how people get promoted. Don't send me your Human Resource, or the new improved name Talent, Department procedures and explain how much better it is on your team. Every horror story discussed is from teams that had plenty of best practices and forms that "proved" they have a good appraisal process. Break out of this standard best practice and use the metrics to perform the appraisal.

If you have gone through the exercise of creating operational and financial metrics and then published to the performance appraisal and reviewed all this with team members, the performance appraisals don't have to be the gut-wrenching experience most managers convey they currently are. They are typically bad because:

- You only do it once a year and you are digging up old things that happened or remember only vaguely.

- You don't have any concrete metrics; therefore, you are doing your appraisal based on feelings. Then, you are justifying your appraisal with whatever evidence you can come up with

- You have a psychotic team member who would behave this way regardless of how you measured them

If you tell a team member they must do X and they don't do X, write it on the performance appraisal. Most sane people will not disagree when you point that out. I said most. If you have a "Reason 3" on your team the good news is that with the metrics in place this can be the last bad experience you have with them in the appraisal process. I never said managing humans on a team was easy.

Actual Performance vs. Statistical Theory

Another major problem with the performance appraisal process is that instead of measuring to metrics teams gravitate to ensuring theirs rating match a stated statistical probability. This includes an almost universal belief in using the Bell Curve theory of measurement for performance. The Bell Curve is the theory that every team has high performers, an almost exact number of low performers, and a much larger statistical middle group of average performers. Since we apparently can't define good metrics and measure performance, the next best thing is to attempt to scientifically rate people based on a statistical model.

Does your team really look like this?

YE OLDE HR BELL CURVE BONUS MODEL

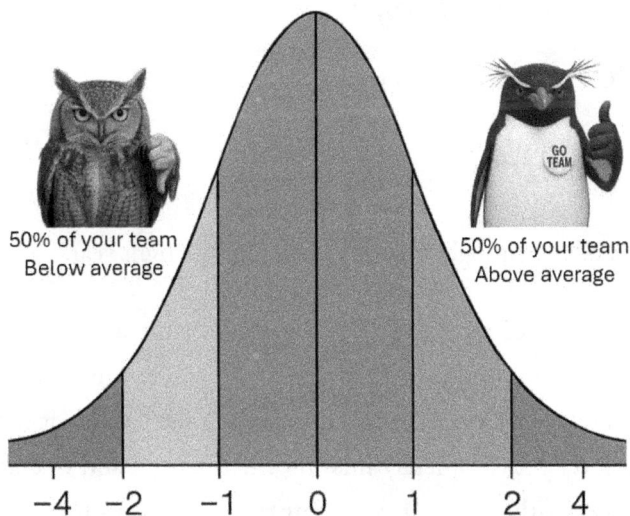

50% of your team
Below average

50% of your team
Above average

−4 −2   −1   0   1   2   4

Is this the type of team you need? I didn't say have right now, but is it what you need? Let me answer for you. No, it is not the team you are looking for. It has just become a religious artifact of the business world because it was passed down through the generations by poor team managers who barely passed their statistics class. If you don't rate your team members like this your boss, who never understood what a real metric was, or HR, will start to notice and wonder if you are being too soft if the ratings skew to the right or worse if the ratings skew to the left.

For example, I had the experience with one manager who admitted to me how he contributed to giving the annual "performance review" such a well-deserved bad name. He started the performance review by telling me that he had eight people and only enough budget money to give one "3" (the highest rating); therefore, he passed it around every year. Others were doing a great job as well, but he needed to be fair and didn't want his boss questioning him on the ratings. How could a team member not get motivated by that speech? This manager followed these steps:

1. Created metrics: How long have you been here?

2. Published them: Told employees how long before they got the high rating.

3. Follow through: Gave the rating in the right year.

What type of metric was it? The votes are in, and this qualifies as a stupid metric. Refer once again to Chapter 6 if you are confused. Here is a clear example of following the process at the individual level yet completely missing the financial and operational objectives of the team. If you want to change team behavior you must throw these systems out the window and gain the trust of your team that you will follow through on performance rewards, IF they earn them.

Some organizations with terrible metrics have taken this Bell Curve approach to measuring team members and added another twist of insanity. The latest fad is to rank everyone and lay off the bottom percentile. To the typical team leader performing a shallow gut analysis, this looks like the silver bullet to a high-performance team. However, the first issue is who does the ranking? If you answered the team leaders that got the team into this mess, you win. The next question is, what do you think are the metrics that will be used for this list? At what team level do you look at the bottom percentile? If you look at the lowest team level, the bottom performer in one group might be your best performer if they were on another team. What was the metric used by the manager to rank them?

The stated purpose of this exercise is to continually raise the bar by firing the low performers and hiring better team members. This reasoning is asinine at best and a lie at worse. It is a lie when you are using it as an excuse to cut salary cost quickly, since the management team has no idea what the problem is and doesn't have time to fix the quarterly results any other way. After it is completed, of course your productivity magically improves. Any idiot can do this, yet it is still heralded as a brilliant management best practice because the team leader who bragged about it and the media reported on it was getting great quarterly results... duh.

For the most dysfunctional and incompetent leadership teams this approach will initially work because chances are you do not have a bell curve but a fat curve of incompetence on the left side of the graph. Are you a member of this type of leadership team?

DYSFUNCTIONAL LEADERSHIP TEAM CURVE

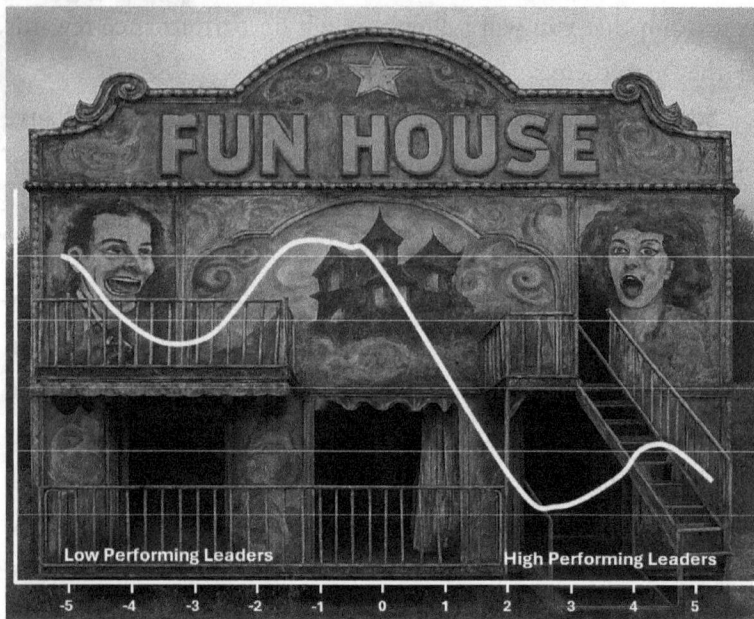

The leaders making the ranking decision, if placed in a team management competency curve, would be on the extreme left. They don't think they are because, after all, they were promoted to management. With this curve if no other changes are made you will have fewer people to get the work done with your dysfunctional process and people causing a downward spiral, but at least it will look like your productivity went up for a while. If you do replace the alleged poor performers with new people, who will you hire? If you have the same management team with bad metrics you get different faces and the same results.

Forget about bell curves and standard human model behaviors. What you need is the Steep Mountain Cliff Team Curve.

STEEP MOUNTAIN CLIFF TEAM CURVE

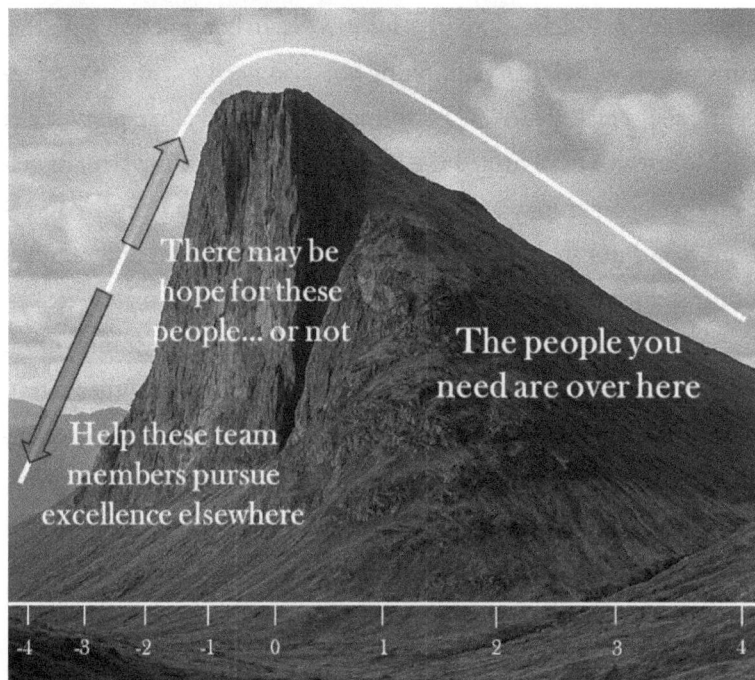

There may be hope for these people... or not

The people you need are over here

Help these team members pursue excellence elsewhere

-4 -3 -2 -1 0 1 2 3 4

Since you don't have a team comprised of students in the government school system or the general population, this is the graph you need. If you have a general population team the only one who should get the low evaluation is you, the leader who created a team full of losers. You should have all good to great performers or get rid of them. Random ten percent headcount reductions demonstrate leadership incompetence, not efficient management.

Remember you do not have to abide by the "No Child Left Behind Act." Let other organizations use a Bell Curve measure. Your job is to remove everyone not meeting job requirements. On a five-point anyone rated less than a "3" should either on their way out or on a short-term improvement plan. This doesn't mean an employee rates as a 3 instantly becomes a 2 because you fired a poor performer. Not if you have well-defined metrics for success. In conjunction with the elimination of Bell Curve thinking you also need to change the perception and reality of a "3" performance rating on a five-point scale.

Most teams have turned the rating of 3 into the equivalent of getting the soccer trophy at the end of the season. You get it by showing up and not making the boss mad. The perception of a ranking of three must be changed to mean good performance in your area as opposed to average. The goal is that average goes to the competition. This can be a terrible struggle when your team sees all the other teams within the organization are celebrating mediocrity instead of meritocracy. Your job as a leader is to create a team that prides itself on achieving real goals and not comparing their performance with the best mediocre-in-class competition. Focus on being the best of the best.

TEAMWORK MOMENT OF TRUTH

A team leader who uses the Bell Curve for appraisals should remove the lowest performer by resigning. The team performance average will immediately go up.

As a team leader you must overcome your bias regarding your own people good or bad due to lack of good metrics to begin with. At every level of the organization I will hear "my people are the best." Any casual outside observer would say "at best" some of your people are "the best." In some cases, the statement is so far removed from reality that I must believe the person is delusional or just lying to avoid being exposed as incompetent. Instead of fixing the problem, we develop a performance appraisal and merit increase policy based on an interpretation of things such as the Bell Curve.

STEP 6: COMPENSATE
BASED ON THE METRICS

Even if the measurement process is followed, the annual appraisal is not used to effectively to drive individual behavior at the compensation level. At worst it is just used to justify whatever raise needs to be given based on predetermined budget numbers from last year—regardless of the team's financial and operational performance. The raise is based on the performance rating that translates into a percentage. That percentage must be split among the team members within the finite salary budget. If everyone who gets an "average" raise is not associated with achieving or exceeding the metrics of success, you have sent the wrong message to the team and will get the average results you deserve.

There's another, more nefarious reason the Bell Curve is used. In many appraisal systems, performance ratings are directly tied to fixed compensation increases. By adopting this statistical model, organizations can more easily forecast salary budgets at the start of the year. Some companies even require team leaders to distribute ratings according to the curve. This approach may seem logical—especially in dysfunctional teams where no one can clearly define what separates great from poor performance in a given role. It also acts as a brake on team leaders who claim all their people are top performers. Without metrics to back up those claims, they often default to giving everyone the highest rating, which ultimately sends the message that excellence is meaningless and going above and beyond isn't worth the effort.

Whatever the rationale for using a simplistic statistical model, it undermines the core principle of performance-based compensation. Pay should be directly tied to operational and financial outcomes—not distributed according to statistical averages. That starts with setting meaningful goals. If your metrics are solid, you should see a clear correlation between performance and compensation. If that link is missing, then the compensation system itself needs to be redesigned to reward actual results. Some team members may believe that merely showing up earns a trophy. That might have worked on their fifth-grade soccer team—but in a high-performing organization, the bar must be higher.

Leaders must define what excellence looks like and how it will be measured. That means rejecting the Bell Curve mentality in both performance appraisals and bonus programs. Even if the budget pool remains fixed, you can recalibrate the distribution—lower the amounts if needed—and reward based on a steep performance curve that reflects real achievement.

On many teams, all things related to performance seem to be dictated by the oracle of people management: the HR department. Like many support functions, HR has become increasingly obsessed with process and system implementation. While well-intentioned, in some cases, this often creates obstacles, inflexibility, and constraints around hiring, managing, and rewarding performance.

These limitations are widely acknowledged by leaders—but they're also frequently used as an excuse to avoid doing the hard work of building a winning team. From my perspective, if you take the initiative to educate yourself, you'll gain the insight needed to make smarter decisions about team building. Regardless of the systems in place, a committed team leader can usually create meaningful goals and performance metrics within those constraints. The key words here are "most of the time."

If your current HR department has successfully built a power base that micromanages every corner of the organization, imposes one-size-fits-all processes, and worships the government-model handbook of compensation rules-good luck. You're in for a long and perilous journey with slim odds of securing additional compensation for a high-performing team member buried under HR job code 42666. The irony? The very HR department that has amassed this level of control doesn't trust the leaders they themselves hired to make sound decisions about managing their own teams.

Compensating your team appropriately is one of the most powerful levers for achieving the results you want. But here's the catch: defining what "appropriate" actually means is hard work. That's why so few leaders bother. It's easier to chase silver-bullet fixes-hand out branded coffee mugs, roll out a shiny new methodology, or install the latest software. But let's be honest: does anyone really believe a sales automation tool creates better salespeople?

When you commit to real metrics, real leadership, and real accountability, something remarkable begins to happen. Your culture starts to shift. People who align with your values and standards will gravitate toward your team. And those who were quietly blocking progress—clinging to respect they "earned" a decade ago—will start to exit. That's when the transformation accelerates. Once positive momentum builds, it compounds. It fuels performance, attracts talent, and grows the business. The not-so-secret ingredient to high-performing teams: you must walk the walk when it comes to accountability and responsibility.

TEAMWORK MOMENT OF TRUTH

If YOU don't hold yourself accountable to help the team, don't expect the team to hold themselves accountable to follow YOU.

Even if your manager doesn't require it, your role is to support your team and help them overcome roadblocks to success. Your role as a mentor is to help—not do it for them. Most people have an idea on how to proceed and just need somebody to discuss their approach and get validation and/or additional suggestions. Then, when the team executes you stand by them. Even if it was wrong, you can still be accepting and supportive when you explain how they might have handled things differently and then move on. Your job is to get the resources and overcome organizational roadblocks they have attempted to remove. Provide whatever support it takes for your team to get it done. If you are not doing these things refer to "YOU are the problem" in Chapter 3. Team management is hard.

CHAPTER 11

THE ENEMIES WITHIN THE TEAM

"If you know the enemy and know yourself you need not fear the results of a hundred battles."

SUN TZU

There are many people on the team who will be excited about the changes you are bringing. They will respond to focusing on the true mission, having concrete objectives to achieve, fair metrics supporting those objectives, the accountability and responsibility, and in general treating individual members of the team as adults. You also will discover people, who other team leaders thought were poor employees, turn into star performers helping the team achieve new levels of success. These people will feed off your energy and you will feed off theirs. Then there will be the others.

Yes, these "team" players will not change no matter what you do. Even if you told them to clap their hands twice or they will lose their job, they would clap once and say that was close enough. Whether afflicted by years of habit, deep-down hatred of their lives, career choices, personal issues, or delusional fantasies they will never, ever, ever, ever, ever, change. There may be some who might consider changing after discovering the benefits of unemployment. Some will finally pursue something else they would like to do because they were lucky enough to be fired by you. This will unlock the golden handcuffs of their own making and not having the courage to leave a job they know is making them miserable. Others will just be angry and bitter, learn nothing, and move on to your competitor. This is your team goal. To "help" them move out voluntarily or evict them from the neighborhood, e.g., the team. If they go to your competitor that is a bonus.

As leader of the team, you have a process to go through when removing a poor performing team member. I am not talking about whatever human resource process that was invented to "exit" an employee. The real process you go through is:

Agonize—Recognize—Categorize—Antagonize—Exorcize

AGONIZE

You executed all the steps towards team success and yet something is wrong. You listened to the team, built the metrics, and you worked hard to incorporate their suggestions into the plan, yet everything is still a struggle. Even when the entire team says they completely agree with you nothing happens. Did you forget to announce the following?

"Hi, I'm the new team leader and there are going to be some really big changes made that should get you excited. To really pump everyone up, here's an awesome coffee mug that says. Teamwork! Yes, we can!!!"

Well, if even the magic Teamwork coffee mug doesn't get the job done it may be because it doesn't matter what you do. It will never happen because there are people on the team who have made it their life's work to ruin whatever idea you or anyone else may have to make things work better. Improve quality, customer satisfaction, or operational performance? It doesn't matter. Their goal is all about maintaining the status quo, and in the process making your job twice as hard regardless of how good your metrics are.

TEAMWORK MOMENT OF TRUTH

It will not matter how much you get input from the team before you make decisions because some people just suck.

Many people want to have a friendly, team-oriented work environment; conflict avoidance is a human characteristic that is a part of many team cultures. When changes are implemented, you proceed to do the right thing and over-communicate. There are change announcements, discussions are encouraged in team meetings, emails sent, procedures and processes are documented, and reminders to everyone to follow them. After an honest review of progress, you discover that things are not getting better.

How can this be? You may then spend many hours agonizing over how to resolve an issue with team performance or why one individual is disrupting the process. This is a very difficult emotion for most team leaders to overcome because deep down they know they are putting off difficult decisions and actions even if they know their life will be easier afterwards. This is compounded when there are team members who you genuinely like or may even be someone you interact with outside of work. Regardless of your personal feelings, at the end of the day you must accept accountability and responsibility to make the change. You owe it to the team to do something about the current situation regardless of the short-term pain and how uncomfortable it makes you. This includes the gauntlet of loops and additional work most companies will insist you do to document poor performance. In the long run you will have less of these tasks to do as your team gets stronger with each person you remove who is hampering the team's ability to be successful.

RECOGNIZE

Now that you're ready to confront the enemies within, you must first identify who they are within the team. Next, categorize why they pose a threat to a successful team dynamic, and then apply the appropriate remedy. Your goal is one of three outcomes:

- Improvement.
- Voluntary leave.
- Termination.

You will encounter resistance, no matter how bad the current working situation is or how much everyone claims to support you. Team leaders often mistake nodding heads in meetings for genuine understanding and agreement. More often, it's just the final stage of a sugar coma.

The opposite mistake is assuming that someone who walks in and appears openly confrontational is your biggest obstacle to achieving team goals. In reality, these direct resisters are often the easiest to address—if you have even a teaspoon of self-confidence in your position. They might even offer valuable ideas for achieving results more efficiently. Some may become your strongest team players, or they might be the first to leave. Either way, you win.

CATEGORIZE

If you've recognized that resistance is inevitable, it's time to categorize that resistance to help chart the appropriate course of action. While your team goals and metrics remain constant, your approach to individual team members matters—not just to motivate the group, but to engage those who have the work ethic, communication skills, sense of responsibility, and knowledge to be effective contributors, if they're focused on the right objectives.

Now, I may be making a bold assumption: that you, the team leader, are capable of adapting your communication style based on the individual. If not, I suggest a bit of autodidactic training in that area. The assumption throughout this book is that you possess some core competencies required to lead a team. Yes, I'm taking a risk with that assumption—but between you and me, it's "them" who are the problem. Correct?

There are the three key categories of resistance to watch out for:

- Aggressive resisters.
- False supporters.
- Special needs.

Aggressive Resisters

These types of resisters can be both overt and subversive. Even the most clueless team leaders usually manage to identify the overt ones. It's the subversive resisters who are far more difficult to weed out. They typically fall into three categories:

- Hard workers who believe you're wrong and refuse to change, no matter what you do.

- Employees who think they've accumulated too much perceived expert power—making them feel exempt from team procedures and goals, often bolstered by a relationship with someone "higher up."

- Individuals with various personality disorders.

Hard-working resisters

They say, "I don't like these changes, and they won't work. I hereby refuse to follow your leadership." This is the easiest group to address—and most managers will find the courage to do so. Why? Because you have no choice. You've been issued a public challenge, and it's now a contest of wills. Give them a choice: stay or go.

Expert power resisters

Expert power resisters are by far the most annoying—yet also the easiest to deal with. Fire them. Hasta la vista, baby.

Do you think I'm kidding? If you allow anyone to believe the team can't function without them, you jeopardize the entire operation. Many expert-power freaks have learned to get their way by acting like bullies. Call their bluff, and some will back down the moment they're written up for failing to meet a specific metric. They'll be shocked and angry, but that smackdown is often enough to inject a healthy dose of reality into the situation.

There's another benefit: you've made a bold statement. I mean what I say and say what I mean. Typically, the "expert" has buffaloed everyone—including your boss—into thinking they're indispensable.

In reality, they're often driven by low self-esteem. They build confidence by becoming technical experts in narrow areas, then guard that knowledge like a dragon hoarding treasure.

Their knowledge isn't that hard to replace—and probably isn't that vast to begin with. They withhold key information, forcing others to rely on them to solve problems. This reinforces their perceived value to upper management. They love making a big deal out of being the go-to person, even though they created the bottleneck by refusing to document processes or share resolutions.

They're not necessarily smarter—they just work hard to keep everyone else "stupid." Many times, they've deliberately hidden information that others could easily access, believing that knowledge is power. And by that, I don't mean the power to improve the team. I mean the power to protect their turf and block any changes that threaten their control.

In one process improvement initiative I worked on, everyone insisted they had to go through a single individual to get the information needed to complete a task. Let's call this team member Bob. When I arrived, people couldn't stop talking about how critical Bob was to the success of a particular project. So I did a quick investigation—and discovered why Bob was considered indispensable. He had created a document that outlined the procedure and included the necessary codes. The catch? It wasn't documented anywhere else. Bob kept this Holy Grail locked in his desk. Yes, you read that correctly. It wasn't hidden in a file on his computer. It was literally locked in a desk drawer, like some old-time bank vault hoarding precious gold nuggets.

Sometimes companies tolerate toxic behavior because they believe they need "experts"—and that such experts are hard to find, so allowances must be made. But no expert is worth that cost.

First, most so-called experts in an organization are simply people who've acquired knowledge about a specific area. While it may appear that their expertise is advancing team goals, what they're often doing is sabotaging the team's long-term success.

The solution to the issue with Bob was to redefine what makes a team member valuable. That meant Bob had to operate under a new set of expectations: documenting key processes, conducting training, and ensuring that information was kept up to date and accessible online. Otherwise, his previous performance rating of 5 would drop to a 2—and there would be no raise. That message shook Bob to the core of his self-perceived value. But over time, he began to see the benefits of letting go of his gatekeeping role.

He came to understand that his value to the team—and his personal rewards—increased as he helped improve overall team performance. Enforced metrics paired with meaningful incentives work better than most people think.

Those with personality disorders

Some people come with "issues"—and lucky you, they've been assigned to your team. New metrics, incentives, and motivational theories won't help here. No matter how strongly HR supports the "no-child-left-behind" philosophy, you must make plans to leave these individuals behind. Far, far behind. Your team cannot be held back because you feel sorry for someone who consistently undermines progress. Put them on the express train off your team.

False Supporters

The most difficult and insidious team member is the passive-aggressive resister—armed with a vast arsenal of subtle tactics designed to undermine any attempt at change. They'll agree to follow processes and procedures, but their actual execution is minimal at best. Worse still, they may engage in sabotage—quietly stirring conflict with other departments, coworkers, or even your boss.

Some of this behavior stems from fear of the unknown. You're changing their world. But another driver is the threat of exposure. Deep down, they know their perceived value hinges on maintaining archaic, convoluted processes that only they understand. If those are stripped away, they become just like everyone else—and subject to the same metrics and accountability.

Don't underestimate how powerful this fear can be, or how it shapes their behavior in a team setting. One common tactic is to claim that change is "hurting the team"—because they want to define what the team is. This rationalization allows them to justify anti-team behavior while appearing loyal to the organization. You'll find yourself scratching your head when you call these individuals in and ask why they're not complying with what seem like the simplest job requirements.

Passive-aggressive false supporters are the most difficult to manage. They'll sit in your office, nod in agreement, and even admit they're struggling—but insist they're "on board" and trying to change. Most managers, in the allegedly cruel world of business, will give these individuals chance after chance simply because they say they believe in the mission. But without true accountability, the entire team begins to question your commitment to change. The real problem? Most people avoid direct confrontation. We sidestep it—even when it's quietly destroying our team, our emotional well-being, and our organization.

Special Needs Employees

Then there are the "special categories"—the boss's nephew, the director's husband from another department, or anyone with a

204 \\ **THERE IS AN i IN TEAM**

protected status that makes them feel untouchable. These are the snakes in the grass who can quietly sabotage your efforts if not handled properly.

Another challenge: team members who simply aren't mentally up to the task. They've survived in the organization by maintaining a facade of competence. Many are genuinely nice people—but that doesn't make them effective contributors. Your goal here is to find a place for them outside your team if you believe they could still add value elsewhere. The worst thing you can do is feel sorry for someone and give them a pass. That message will destroy whatever credibility you've built with the true performers on your team.

The charismatic yet incompetent

Chad Dazzling is one of your team members who's dynamic, passionate, speaks well, and creates stunning presentations. The only problem? Chad has never followed through or performed in his actual role. It's clear he belongs on the list of those to be set free—to pursue excellence elsewhere. The real challenge comes when your boss says, "I just had a meeting with Chad Dazzling on your team. What a great presentation and such a dynamic personality. Maybe we should fast-track him to a leadership position."

Do not underestimate the power of The Chad Effect. It infects every level of an organization—starting with HR recruiting and hiring. The danger escalates as you move up the leadership chain, culminating in boardrooms selecting CEOs based on charm rather than competence.

To help you spot a Chad in the wild, here is a useful chart to reference:

Spotting a Chad in the Wild

Charisma is not competence. Here's how to
tell the difference before it's too late.

RED FLAG	WHAT IT LOOKS LIKE	WHY IT'S DANGEROUS
🎤 Presentation over substance	Delivers dazzling updates with zero follow-through	Creates illusion of progress while problems fester
🚀 Promoted on "potential"	Gets fast-tracked despite thin results	Undermines meritocracy and demoralizes actual performers
🧹 Leaves messes behind	Others must fix their mistakes	Erodes team trust and accountability
☺ Universally liked rarely challenged	No one wants to "be the bad guy"	Avoids scrutiny while real issues go unaddressed
♣ Always "networking," never executing	Shows up everywhere except where the work is	Distracts leadership with charm while dodging responsibility

I remember working hard to suppress my initial reaction when a board member discussed the recent selection of a new CEO: "Yes, we're a little concerned about his lack of executive experience and accomplishments... but he's got passion. And when he speaks, it's mesmerizing." Really? That was the criteria? What could possibly go wrong?

As shocking as it is to believe, a lot did go wrong over the next couple of years for that team—including strategic drift, morale erosion, a spike in bipolar egomaniac behavior, and a trail of unaddressed issues. Charisma without competence isn't leadership—it's theatre. And when the curtain falls, it's the team left sweeping up the mess.

These internal enemies—whether they're coasting, connected, or simply incapable—must be managed across, down, or out. You do this through the financial and operational objectives you've established, and by enforcing them with clear metrics. The moment you start making excuses, you're finished. Those who believed in your approach will lose respect for you as a leader, and your results will erode over time. Yes, these resistors will hate you. They'll hate your metrics, and they'll hate accountability.

Get over it. If you need more friends, join a bird-watching club after work. It's far better than watching these birds chirp all day and get nothing done.

ANTAGONIZE

The following approach assumes you've followed all the steps in the previous chapters around Financial and Operational metrics. This assumption matters for two reasons:

1. It absolves me of any responsibility for your failure when you inevitably try to blame me for suggesting this approach.

2. This process will turn ugly.

If you don't have solid metrics in place expect difficult conversations with HR and your boss. Expect four times the number of belligerent meetings and unproductive, circular chats with team members. And yes—expect to question your own sanity. Especially when your boss says, "I just spoke with Chad Dazzling. He's worried about his position on the team. Are you sure he's part of the problem?" Yes, boss. I'm very sure he's a problem. You could add, "That statement just helped me identify another reason why we're in this mess." And while that's probably true, saying it out loud might be a career-limiting move—at least if you plan to stay on his team.

The good news is that if you follow the steps outlined in this book, most team members will understand how they got there. They may disagree or tell you they were too busy with a crisis; however, those are entirely different conversations.

I have made some pointed critiques about the state of HR in today's team environment— especially the growing influence and power that, frankly, hasn't translated into higher-performing teams. But here's the flip side: Most HR employee problems stem from team leaders who refuse to do the upfront work. They avoid setting clear goals and defining measurable objectives. They then proceed to ignore non-compliance, either out of laziness or fear of confrontation.

In the end? They get more confrontations than they ever would by simply inserting a logical and measurable goal into an objective—and then applying responsibility fairly, regardless of personal preferences.

The other goal is self-selection. In most cases, when behavior isn't improving the employee begins to self-select off the team. That's the goal. When someone refuses to change, and knows you are serious about removing them, many will start looking for another job, either outside the company or in a different department. This outcome usually only works when all the steps are applied appropriately in advance. This enables most people with normal intelligence to figure out what's coming if they've chosen not to follow your leadership. And yes, the key words here are "normal intelligence."

You'll encounter a wide range of reactions when you begin to enforce true performance metrics. Some team members will show outward acceptance, compliance, and even enthusiasm. Others will be hostile—masking resistance with passive-aggressive behavior. There's only one way to manage them out: Real metrics based on the building blocks of team success.

The reason so many non-performers linger on teams? Outdated rules and lack of accountability for what actually matters in each role. Some people will change, other can't, and some won't—even if they know how. They liked the way it used to be and want that world back. The introduction of new metrics disrupts every task they've clung to-sometimes for over twenty years. It doesn't matter that if you had a time machine and went back twenty years you would find they were complaining about everything even then, in the so-called "good old days." Do you think a training class in teamwork is going to override twenty years of on-the-job training in accountability avoidance? Go right ahead and try. Then come back to this chapter for what actually works.

TEAMWORK MOMENT OF TRUTH

The journey of a thousand miles begins with a single step. That step is easier if you remove the boat anchor tied to your leg.

Your first step as a leader is to change your thought pattern. Your team must be competitive to stay in business. They need to strive to be the best at their function to achieve that objective. And your people need to be the best they can be as individuals and as contributors to the team. Instead, we continue dragging around boat anchors. Why? Because no one bothered to hold those anchors accountable. In some cases, we're not just dragging one anchor, we are towing an entire boat full of them behind our ship. If the metric is to keep the team from succeeding, then make that the official metric and give the boat anchors a bonus, Otherwise, do something about.

EXORCISE

Let's get started removing all the enemies from within! Step one: state the obvious. Just about every organization has some type of HR policy that outlines a disciplinary process. That doesn't mean it is followed or even remotely effective. Even with a solid policy in place its application is often wildly inconsistent across divisions, departments, and job title. So regardless of what is written in the HR Dead Sea Scrolls, here's a course of action for any people "improvement" process.

You have been outlining metrics. You've supported your team, coached them, and it is not working. It is now time for the five-step program that I'll outline here. Yes, it will be difficult but consider the alternative. If you don't institute this five-step program for recalcitrant team members, in just a couple of years you will have to enter the ten-step program at Alcoholics Anonymous. That will be the only way to save yourself after dealing with these idiots for too long. It's time to deploy the "Exit Ramp Protocol" on our Team Autobahn in order to clear the road of poor performing transport vehicles.

THE EXIT RAMP PROTOCOL

Step 1: The Verbal Warning

This is the "Hey, you are not following the process outlined for your position" moment. It's direct and it's clear. This step only works for those who are truly committed, especially early on when they're just wrestling with changing bad habits. They'll take the conversation seriously and course-correct. Here is the critical part. Always pair the verbal warning with a written follow-up. This is not optional. It builds your paper trail and protects you from the HR no-child-left-behind department that might try to derail disciplinary action later. Why document?

- Tracks employee performance over time
- Clarifies expectations and next steps
- Shields you from HR interference driven by lawsuit paranoia

Let's be honest: HR isn't always protecting employees—they're protecting process. They love being the gatekeepers of the sacred,

overly complicated ritual of termination. Why? Because they're terrified of lawsuits from 1-800-looter-lawyer.com. But here's the truth:
you can't prevent lawsuits. No amount of documentation will stop
someone from filing a ridiculous claim. In fairness, HR's paranoia is
partly earned. Too many bad managers gave bad performers endless
passes. Now, when someone finally holds a poor performer accountable, it looks like "bullying." Especially if that person was a "superstar" last year. That's why you start early—show they're not meeting
objectives in this role over time.

Verbal warnings are underused. You don't have to jump to any
other step to use them. You can have a few or several depending on
the infraction. Just be careful: "several" shouldn't turn into infin-
ity. Bad leaders give 100 verbal warnings and do nothing. In some
cases, this is followed by handing out "exceeds expectations" ratings
because the employee showed up occasionally and the team leader
didn't want conflict.

Make the number of warnings appropriate and don't hide behind
slack messages or emails. Yes, electronic notices are fast and convenient, but many times they are also a great way to avoid face-to-face
conflict. It is surprising the number of leaders I have worked with
that also believe written communications leave no room for interpretation. Humans are masterful mind-readers. They'll invent entire
emotional backstories behind your written tone. So have the conversation first, then document it. You won't eliminate misinterpre-
tation, but you'll minimize it.

The "Verbwritten" Follow-Up: After the verbal warning, send a
casual written note to reinforce the message. Something like:

"Hey, I appreciate our conversation today and understand you
didn't realize the expectation was to actually do work while at work.

I appreciate your commitment to now doing the work assigned when you're here. Thanks!"

This "Verbwritten" warning sets the stage for the next step. It's your receipt. Your timestamp. Your proof that the issue has been addressed.

Step 2: The Written-Verbal

While a verbal warning can be a quick conversation followed up with an email or message, the written-verbal is a more deliberate step. It's where you sit down with the person, explain the behavior, and outline exactly what they need to do to correct it. Then you follow up with a written recap of the conversation and the required action. This is the most critical, yet often overlooked, step in resolving performance issues. Too many leaders skip straight to formal write-ups. If you're driving major change and want to give good employees a real shot at success, this step is essential. It also eliminates the classic first line of defense: "What? I was never told! I'm shocked! This feels like it came out of nowhere!". This step will not, of course, eliminate this claim from your more psychotic team members. But it will give them something they can't argue with: evidence that the conversation happened in the real world. That evidence matters. It removes "Lack of Knowledge" or "misunderstanding" as excuses and clears the path for accountability.

Step 3: The Formal Write-Up

The formal write-up builds on the previous write-up and the verbal warning. In many ways it is not dramatically different than the first verbal write-up-except for one critical shift. You are now putting the employee on notice that the next step is probation and possible termination if the behavior isn't corrected. Occasionally, this is where the fog finally lifts for some team members. Your aggressive experts who believe the business can't run without them, and your passive-aggressive people who refuse to change should already be quietly exploring other opportunities, inside and outside the organization. That's not a problem. That's progress. Depending on the situation, the formal write-up is the right moment to make your stance unmistakably clear: Significant improvement is required and failure to meet expectations will result in probation or termination. This isn't about punishment. It's about clarity, accountability, and protecting the integrity of the team.

Step 4: Probation

Probation is typically a 90-day period during which the employee must shape up or be terminated. Some people seem to think that gives them up to 90 days to start fixing the problem. I've "enjoyed" leading employees who were written up multiple times, placed on probation, and then on termination day said, "Hey wait I thought I had ninety-days of probation." No Mr. Teamwork Guy. As explained to you at the beginning, and multiple times in writing, it is really like prison probation in reverse. In prison probation one violation sends you back to prison. Here, one violation sends you out-released from our team to roam the world in search of new adventures and organizations better suited to your "teamwork" abilities. And the cool part? It doesn't matter if it is day one or day eighty-nine. We take you off probation.

If you work for HR, please skip the following sentence. At this point a team leader's goal is not redemption—it is termination. That should be your mindset. Redemption ended after the employee exhibited same behavior after the formal write-up. Yes, there have been cases where probation has worked. There has also been multiple sighting of Sasquatch. And by "worked" I don't mean someone who managed to stay out of trouble for 90-days. There are plenty of people who have mastered the art of gaming the HR systems. I mean someone who went on probation for a legitimate, work-related reason—then turned things around and became a top-performing team member. Those cases are rare.

Of course, not every organization operates the same way. Some organizations may define probation as a guaranteed 90-day runway. Others are bound by union contracts or government entity rules. So yes-your milage may vary. Nevertheless, in most organizations across various industries, you can legally set people free at the next problem or, as they say in the HR business, the next occurrence. Isn't that a nice way of putting it? So polite. So gentle. Because heaven forbid, we hurt anyone's feelings.

Step 5: Set Them Free

Yes, no matter what you do and how long it takes, some people will not change. It is time to set them free. If you have followed all the stages outlined here this will not be as stressful as it would seem. The real problem with firing someone isn't HR. It's that managers don't want to make the hard decision to start the process. They hope the problem will magically go away.

There are several reasons contributing to this wish:

- You like the person as an individual.

- Deep down you are a romantic and you think everyone can be saved, even from themselves.

- You feel guilty about someone losing their income and blame yourself.

- Fear of repercussions from firing the brother in-law of an executive.

- You're lazy.

- You are a fan of conflict avoidance.

These are the real reason, not the HR processes, that keep leaders from firing people on the team. If you follow the process outlined here, which is set up to avoid legal issues, there are few HR departments that will stand in your way. I didn't say they will make it easy, just that eventually they will acquiesce to the final departure from Gate 6. One major exception to this is a team member who is either related to or liked by the person leading Human Resources or another executive. Even then you've got a decent shot at getting them transferred to another team. While this is not ideal for the overall team, sometimes you must just concern yourself with making your high school clique better.

Most terminated employees, except for the truly dysfunctional personality types, won't be surprised when the day comes. There will always the few dysfunctional, or just reality impaired, team members who after being warned multiple times, written up, and put on probation will act shocked when they are terminated from the team. One of my favorite reactions of all time: "What? I thought I had the full 90 days on probation before I had to start complying with the metrics." Well, you "thought" wrong. The good news, at least for us, is the truth will set you free—at least from this team.

On a truly dysfunctional team you will need to award several deserving candidates their ticket to freedom before the entire team gets an important message: unlike the past 2,000 change events, this one is the real deal. What follows are some real challenges from actual teams attempting to make meaningful change. The names have been changed to protect the guilty, and occasionally the delusional. So, if you're knee-deep in resistance, passive aggression, or outright chaos created by some of your team members take heart. You're not alone. Others have gone where few team leaders have boldly gone before. And lived to tell the tale.

Handling the indispensable expert

Meet Janice. She's a software developer who keeps the accounting system running, or so she says. She tells everyone how she's constantly "saving the day", always how she must stop what she's doing to help with a tough problem. She has become a legend in her own mind. All this self-promotion has somehow permeated into the minds of senior leadership who now think she is a superstar— especially technically illiterate senior leaders who view her work as somewhat mystical. She is willing to help if people prostrate themselves before her and affirm her brilliance. She also takes every opportunity to express "concerns" to the team leader about the technical ability of coworkers. Janice paints herself as the lone genius surrounded by mere mortals on her team, yet somehow, she gets the job done. Some on the team believe that she is an expert because they don't understand the code. Other team members figured out that if they grovel Janice will take on the task of fixing the problem. Meanwhile, she is whispering to the boss about how she saved the day once again on a project.

Welcome to metric world, Janice! The key is to not just have a metric that Janice did something. Maybe it is time to ask some questions. Is it a good outcome that Janice created a program that breaks every month when payroll is run? Is it healthy that no one can figure out how to debug the Spaghetti code except the genius who wrote it, that is, Janice? Is it acceptable that there is zero documentation on how the code works if Janice gets sick, or walks out? Was the goal to create an application with no quality metrics and an increase in support costs for your team? If the client thinks the program is unstable is Janice really a superstar?

Time for a new set of metrics for Janice. Her old metric was how many bugs she fixed every month on a program she created. Her new metric is to fix the application to make it stable and provide the ability for others to debug and fix. You can really go crazy and include a client satisfaction metric on application reliability. In some cases, your own "Janice" will prove she is a superstar and make it happen. What this particular Janice did was first attempt to undermine the team leader with her boss. When this didn't work, she refused, or was incapable, of meeting the metrics. In the end she threatened to quit and then she actually did to punish the company for not appreciating her importance.

The result? The rest of the development team was immediately motivated to prove they were not the idiots Janice said they were and improved both the reliability and documentation of the application. In the meantime, all that bad behavior was relocated to another team, which thought they had won a big prize. What you have done is given a virus to the competition, which, over time will make them weak and you stronger!! The best self-selection outcome is Win–Win.

Just remember this quote when a team member starts thinking they can't be replaced:

> *"The cemeteries are full of indispensable men."*
> CHARLES DE GAULLE

And yes, that includes Janice, your executive team, and for that matter, even you.

The cheerleading project manager

Another example is Bill the Project Manager, who has convinced management how great he is. After all, he is "certified." Yes, certifiably bad. His specialty is creating colorful weekly status reports, building complicated risk assessments, and networking skills. Now, let's peel back the curtain.

No project that Bill works on ever comes in on time, or on budget. Most are disasters, yet Bill effectively transfers blame to IT development, training, or the client. Bill is very articulate and has a command of the most arcane project management buzzwords. Bill's Vice President buys into Bill's shtick because it helps absolve him too. It is an insidious, repeatable process.

It's metric time Bill! First, tell Bill he now owns the outcome for projects he is assigned. His bonus and salary review depend on actual delivery as opposed to optics. Client satisfaction also matters in defining a successful outcome. You also remove the success metric of how dazzling his presentations are.

The PM certifications suddenly don't matter. The first review of the project provides Bill with a verbal warning. After going through the process, Bill was let go because, in fact, he did not possess any of the project success skills his certification supposedly conferred on him. It simply confirmed he had passed a test and paid a fee.

If you are worried that you must replace Bill or don't want to hassle with the hiring process or explain to the boss why you are "hard" on such a "valuable" employee, then sit back and wallow in mediocrity. If no one cares, there is a high probability that there will be major layoffs down the road because you, and your superiors, have no idea how to manage a team. As the team leader you can say all these process and metrics matter, but you must show they matter. Verbal, Written, Probation, Goodbye Bill.

The connected manager

What about the informal org chart? The one that doesn't show up in HR systems but runs the place like a high school cafeteria. This is another insidious roadblock to success for a team. They are the dukes and duchesses in grade school and high school environments. They don't need authority-they have adjacency. They're "plugged in", "well connected", and "untouchable".

Take James. He reports to you, but everyone knows he's "close" to your boss and Jesse, the senior vice president that makes him bullet-proof. The word on the street is don't bother James because Jesse has his back. If you try to change anything you will be gone long before James is. Most managers immediately accept this fact and proceed to work around him. You, on the other hand recognize the truth. There are two problems: below and above. Metrics to the rescue. First, present your department's performance plan to Jesse. She'll love it. Metrics sound responsible and strategic. Loop your boss in too, framing it as a way to make the team a top contributor to her success. You have just started down the road of neutralizing James's protected species status. Slightly devious? Yes. Need for political finesse? Of course! But mostly, it requires courage and conviction to create a plan and make it happen.

Now get busy. Let James know the criteria for success and that you expect everyone on the team to achieve these goals. James does not care because of years of no accountability. He feels that he is untouchable due to his relationship with Jesse. What James doesn't know is that his new boss believes in having good "I's" on the team and plans to do something about reaching that goal. When James doesn't respond you update your boss, and also go to Jesse and say something like: "I know you and James are close. James has mentioned his personal relationship with you, and I want to ensure that you believe the metrics apply to everyone, including James."

While some people may claim this is a devious tactic, it's not. It's direct. You are asking the question everyone's afraid to ask: "Does James actually have to follow the metrics because of his relationship with you?" These conversations are difficult to have and are not without risk. You must address this conversation based on the type of relationship you have with Jesse as well. From personal experience and observations of people using this approach, most employees are usually overstating the extent of the relationship they have with a senior leader to gain clout.

I have seen examples of this with employees who always find a way to talk about how plugged in they are with a senior leader who they either report to or an executive running a different area. They make comments such as I stopped by Ryan's house last weekend, who lives in my neighborhood. Nothing subtle about that hint of referent power. Another way to use this is to look plugged in by implying you are in the know about something such as the statement; "I just saw Jennifer at the club we are both members of. She told me there are some big things are coming." These are all tactics to use referent power to become untouchable.

In this case Jesse didn't want to look like she was covering up for poor performance. James didn't have the backing he thought he did, and people were just afraid to confront him because of the implied relationship. Faced with excellent metrics James was now forced to either comply or leave. James left the team. Unfortunately, it wasn't to another company. He went to another clique at the high school. While conceptually this is bad for the overall team, in this case the leader could only effect change over what she controlled. If you have a James and discover James really is protected, you have a decision to make. It may be time for you to find a different employer or another team at your high school musical. Of course, you can always become one of "them."

TEAMWORK MOMENT OF TRUTH

If you love a team sometimes you must set someone free.

THE TEAM BENEFITS OF SETTING SOMEONE FREE

I have not witnessed a team where the members do not know who is pulling their weight. I have witnessed plenty of team leaders who don't know, or won't make the right decision, to remove individuals who are non-performers from the team. This disconnect regarding the value of certain individuals on a team relates directly back to the lack of accountability through operational and financial metrics.

Free one ineffective chief, vice president, director, or manager who does not achieve the financial and operational objectives that have been set out and you are setting the right tone. Free one team member who everyone knows is a poor performer, but has been here "forever," and everyone on the team takes notice. However, when you set someone free who is meeting the objectives and keep your friends or show loyalty to a long-term employee who you raised to three levels above their level of incompetence, you send a different message. This message says you are not serious about meeting objectives, and you are still an adolescent playing with your friends in high school. The only difference is you have a leadership title like CEO or vice president.

The wonderful thing about the people you need on your team is that what you need to succeed is available. There is no reason to settle for the poor performers you have now when there are other people who will make a significant difference on your team. You just need to go get them. Congress and/or the alphabet soup of regulator entities have not yet demanded that companies are banned from discriminating against lazy people. They have also not stopped the ability to remove people who refuse to adhere to the financial and operational standards you put in place. Well, at least not yet.

There are no executive orders stating that lazy people must be employed. The point is you may have convinced yourself that you can't get rid of poor performers but that is a box of your own making. Show me a place that says they can't fire poor performers, and I will show you a team that does not have the right metrics and procedures in place. Besides, how do you know if someone really is a poor performer if you don't give them a measurement and then reward accordingly? A word of caution. In organizations with a long history of bad behavior it may take more than one or two people departing, especially on a team with a long history of this type of behavior. It takes patience, coaching, and more coaching. Give people a chance, mentor, and then finally tough love. Say goodbye.

CHAPTER 12

HIRING FOR MEASURABLE RESULTS

"However beautiful the strategy,
you should occasionally look at the results."

WINSTON CHURCHILL

You have spent countless hours developing a high-performing team. The individuals on the team now understand the goals and objectives and why these matter to them. Metrics are in place to measure performance; you are now on your way to success. Expansion or the loss of a team member now requires you to hire a new team member. If you want to destroy any momentum you have gained, just follow the standard practices used in most organizations for hiring people. Tell Human Resources to look for people with a four-year degree, confirm the alleged experience and their success as stated in the self-serving advertisement known as a résumé, conduct a one-hour interview, and then choose the "best" candidate to take on the position. What could possibly be easier? There are thousands of books, articles, and case studies on effective hiring you could read. Hundreds of consultants you could pay obscene hourly rates to deliver a "process" as well. You can even install that shiny HR application that promises to take you to the hiring promised land increasing your odds of success. The other option is to just read this chapter before embarking on that expensive journey. The odds are your results will be better. And even if they're not, you'll save a boatload of money and still end up in the same place.

First, let's start with the appetizer of hiring, yes, the résumé. It is considered the first qualifier of technical abilities and alleged experience; it opens the employment gate or Dante's first level of hell experience for you. The French word résumé sounds sophisticated, but the real definition? "Self-serving statement of qualifications." If résumé sounds impressive then I suggest you ask people for their *cheval de fumier*, since that is also French, sounds sophisticated, and is closer to what you typically receive—horse manure.

TEAMWORK MOMENT OF TRUTH

A résumé has never created teamwork or completed any project tasks successfully, so don't hire one.

How do you hire quality candidates if the résumé doesn't help you determine anything about the most important components for team success? You must make the hiring process a journey to find the right individuals who will contribute to team success. Admit it, you just went "duh." Well, if you just thought duh, how did all those idiots ever get hired and stay employed on your team in the first place? There are thousands of books on interviewing techniques, personality tests, and other ways of attempting to determine what makes a good employee. The challenge is that reading books and performing practical application in the real world are unconnected endeavors. Most organizations can also point to their extensive documentation on best practices that enable them to hire the best candidates. They have also hired an army of "talent" experts. If only documented procedures matched the reality of who is hired. If we consider all the attention paid to HR in the last thirty years, the studies, the dissertations, and the books on hiring, how is it possible that anyone is hired who isn't "a good fit?"

One possible reason is you have millions of people who need jobs in order to collect paychecks and will do and say anything to get the job, even if the job will make them miserable and turn them into agents for your competition. No matter what clever cutting-edge technique you come up with, people will figure out how to game your technique to get that paycheck. You also have unions, government entities, media outlets, and a large percentage of the population that believe jobs are the ends to the means as opposed to the means to an end. This really means they think your team is "responsible" to not only create employment, but to keep people employed regardless of contribution. Add to this the latest requirement being propagated that jobs should be "fun."

Yes, I understand there are people who think we have now transcended 5,000 years of how people defined work, and it now needs to be fun. First, don't assume you have a fun organization just because you as a senior team leader decided something would be fun. I am sure all your team members agree that activities such as a mandatory after-work video call social hour or Hawaiian shirt day on Friday are super fun and build great teamwork. After all, the boss came up with the great team-building idea. You should also not trust your enthusiastic Assistant Marketing Director of Employee Engagement

Content when he tells you how much fun the company is to work at. Good luck understanding how "fun" is defined by every employee and potential candidate looking at your job posting that says your company is a fun place to work.

That is bad enough. Now factor in lawyers, who look at organizations as entities with loot for the taking. If the company "lied" about this being a fun job, insist on the new employee doing the actual work they were hired for, and demand employees show up to work when it isn't 'convenient,' what choice does your team member have? They might decide to find one of those altruistic lawyers who promise a plaintiff they won't have to pay a dime for their help and take the not-so-fun team they joined to court. This activity is supported by government entities that encourage this type of behavior because they are looking out for "the people."

A cynical person may observe that most of the people in government passing these lawyer-friendly laws are also lawyers and get campaign funding from other lawyers. I'm shocked when some people suggest that this whole enterprise isn't necessarily in place to help the people against the powerful. One thing that is certain is that this causes organizations to hire more lawyers and compliance employees to the team to add processes and procedures to protect their loot from the other looters for a "small" fee. At this point you begin to wonder why anyone would consider hiring people at all.

The whole process becomes a game, starting with perspective employees trying to hide any known faults and saying whatever needs to be said to secure the job. This is coupled with teams that have job descriptions that contain required functions and skill sets that most of the current team members don't have. Then mix in the fact that companies are lying to the prospective employee about how great the team is as much as the person is misrepresenting how much of a "Team Player" they are. Now combine that with job descriptions that don't match the job people are doing, because someone figured out if you add a certain requirement the job will be graded at a higher or lower pay level. This is followed by extensive documented procedures for hiring that don't address the actual quality of the candidates.

Mix all these inputs together and it certainly sounds like ingredients for a torturous gauntlet for any team leader foolish enough to attempt to find a successful applicant. Half of these steps are in place only because the team has giant roadblocks for removing nonperformers after you let them in the door. Of course, in a partial defense of Human Resources, many of these roadblocks are due to organizational leadership incompetence, no effective metrics in place, and emotionally unstable people allowed to stay in leadership roles.

There are hundreds of books on how to get hired, followed by hundreds of books on interviewing, which tell you what the hiring books are saying. Studying these books can help "normal" people pass through the hiring gauntlet. After a while the process just becomes a series of "gotcha" questions and a Human Resources Manager, aka Personnel Administrator, following a checklist list in the hopes you are not letting in a "bad" candidate. Drug tests, personality tests, and credit checks are implemented because some study somewhere showed statistically that the people who clear these tests might end up as better hires. Unfortunately, there is no test to sniff out the "lazy" drug in the candidate's bloodstream. Due to the threat of lawsuits, you can't really verify what is on the résumé. If you call a previous manager regarding an applicant, they will refer you to "HR," if they even call you back. The HR department at the other company will just confirm "yes, that person worked here." If the candidate does their job the résumé will magically match what your alleged technical requirements are.

Technology has also entered the hiring process, with machine learning applications, aka AI, now being used to scan résumés to look for key attitudes and reject résumés that do not meet the alleged qualifications to sit in front of one of your computer screens. This is another interesting productivity improvement from HR. It is really nothing more than a faster way to look at bogus degrees and credentials as important qualifications, along with key words in the fictional short story written by the candidate. Our $5 million dollar HR system with built with Artificial Intelligence can now scan more than one million applications, giving us the best candidates! This has enabled our team to record a productivity savings of 500%. Of course you saved this much. After all the graph on the PowerPoint presentation shows a steep curve upwards and next to it the statement, "500% Productivity Gain," is in bright green with a great looking font. What more proof does an executive need of a successful implementation?

After going through all the pre-screening, the next steps are interviews by managers and team leaders who have no concept of what a good hire looks like. They confuse smooth talking with communication skills and degrees from prestigious colleges and impressive sounding previous jobs with actual knowledge and work. All in the elusive pursuit of never letting a bad team member join the team. The more work you do upfront because everyone is afraid of having to discipline and then fire someone, the more you are rewarded by the laws of diminishing returns for all this effort. Are you tired yet?

The good news is there are steps you can take to minimize the number of mistakes you make to keep your team at the high-performance level you have worked so hard to achieve. You must first accept that no matter how good you are at hiring the occasional bad apple will get in. There are many liars, self-deluded, sociopaths, chronically lazy, unproductive humans who have the most important certification to pass an interview. This is the coveted CTBSD Certification, otherwise known as the Certified Theatrical Bull-Spewing Self-Delusional Certification. Resign yourself to the reality that you can't ever eliminate letting in idiots and non-performers. Then you can stop wasting precious time and resources attempting to reach hiring nirvana. Realize your team really put all these processes in place because Human Resources and Legal have two lofty goals. They want to be in control of something important to show value and they are terrified of the possibility of firing someone. Of course, most team leaders never want to go through the stressful duty of firing someone either. Since you are reading this book, you now understand it is when, not if, you will ask a team member to seek excellence elsewhere. When that promising new-hire becomes a bad team member review Chapter 10 and throw that rotten apple out of the tree.

TEAMWORK MOMENT OF TRUTH

Nothing could be simpler than hiring a team member except that nothing can be harder.

There are three keys to hiring success:

- Know what you really need.
- Fulfill the need not a position.
- Correct your mistakes.

Each of these keys may sound simple but they are extraordinarily difficult to apply. Many say, few do. If you really want to make a difference you must commit yourself to making it work.

STEP 1: KNOW WHAT YOU REALLY NEED

Of course, you know what you really need. You need a programmer, or marketing director, chemical engineer, auto mechanic, or any one of a million different skills. The problem is that a résumé and an interview are typically the only support of the person's claim she can do the job required. When you add inherent bias into the equation, such as you believe a good talker means a good worker, a young person means go-getter, or a seasoned veteran can't learn new methods, you are painting yourself into a corner based on hearsay and conventional wisdom. You may need specific knowledge and a technical skill. The problem is hiring for just a technical skill could end up wrecking your team. Always remember there are many psychotic people who possess some of the "technical" skills you need. By all accounts Dr. Jekyll was an excellent physician. The key here is that more than anything else you must work hard to increase your percentage of adding the right people to your team. This starts with the people described in Chapter 7 who:

- Demonstrate a strong work ethic.
- Will take ownership and accountability.
- Are metric driven.
- Fulfill whatever technical aspects are required of the position or can learn them.

The first three skills can't be taught. They can be a part of a team member's innate makeup or a behavior which a person doesn't always exhibit yet resolves to accomplish. You can also help bring out these characteristics with metrics and incentives to reach goals. If a person doesn't have the desire, or the mental composition, ordering them to attend a class or reading a book called *Work Ethic for Morons* will not increase performance. These first three traits are the first thing you should be looking for as opposed to starting the conversation with statements such as, 'I need a Certified Project Manager, or I need an Application Developer.'

The Technical Requirements of the Job

There are two parts to the technical requirements that you need to articulate and look for to be successful in your hiring journey:

- Communication skills.
- Specific job skills.

Communication skills

Technical skills are defined as skills that can be taught. Communication also falls into that category. Even the stereotyped technical person who appears to have less than stellar communication skills can learn to improve them—if they want to improve. When you are hiring you are looking for people who can communicate effectively. The ability to communicate is sometimes confused with the ability to interview or the ability to talk. Interviewing is a subset of communications. It does not mean the person can communicate with a team or other stakeholders the team requires to reach their objectives. Talking without listening is a dangerous trait to have in an effective team member. Many poor performers can be eliminated in the hiring process just by keeping this fact in mind as you build the interview process.

Communication is a fundamental skill required for every position on a team. This is your number one job with technical skills; to get people who can communicate and who are also skilled. Communications is a skill that everyone talks about, complains about, and then hires communication consultants to "fix." If you really aren't serious, as exhibited in your own communication skills, save yourself a lot of money and don't hold the communication team-building classes.

Unfortunately, compromising on this skill with your new hires translates into a journey to team failure. When I say communication skills, I'm not talking about acting like a high-energy salesperson on a home shopping channel, or a charismatic social media influencer pitching products. It is the ability to articulate and reach out to the teams' clients, departments, managers, and peers to understand what they are saying and reach agreements and/or understanding on whatever the topic is. A team member must be able to listen effectively. They must also be capable of writing well-crafted emails, communicating appropriately via instant messages, using voice mails, and knowing what communication channel to use and when to use it. Being able to empathize with the other person's point of view is also key to getting the job done. You can hire the most brilliant people in the world and other than bragging about having the most brilliant people in the world you won't get anything done. If they can't communicate, what exactly are you basing your opinion on anyway? Maybe it is based on that diploma hanging on their wall? Maybe you should be deciding based on the value they are generating for the team instead.

Specific technical skills

What are the technical requirements of the position? Do you really need a PhD in Strategic International Finance to process loans? Of course not, yet sometimes that's who gets the job based on what you value and because you told the AI model that having a PhD is the preferred skill set.

There are reasons technical skills are the last thing you should look for. For most jobs you can always find a person who knows how to use a tool. I didn't say you will like the current salary market rate for that person, just that they are available. Maybe you think you need not just someone who can use a hammer, but a CHSS, Certified Hammer Swinging Specialist, who has five years of two-pound red handled hammer experience. They may be in short supply. However, you can hire someone who knows how to hammer, communicates well, and has the desire and will to learn how to use a two-pound red handled hammer. While they may not have that coveted CHSS Certificate on their resume, their ability to do the job you need done is easier to learn than conventional wisdom dictates. The other reason is if they have the first three components, along with the mental ability to quickly learn skills, you will more likely achieve success faster even with the additional time the new employee needs for training to get up to speed on a particular tool, application, or process.

The devolution of the degree as an indicator of success

What specific job skills do you need? If you said a four-year degree, an MBA, or certified purple belt training, those are not skills. They confer a piece of paper and you were not paying attention when this was discussed in Chapter 7. A degree is at best an indicator that a team member might have acquired the ability to understand the terminology of a particular methodology. If you're lucky the candidate had a class or school project on the skill you really need. If the skill you are looking for is a PhD in Ergonomic Design, this is confusing a potential indicator of having some useful knowledge with the actual ability to apply useful knowledge to solve a problem. You need to forget your bias towards perceived expert talent and think about the actual skills required. The ability to start and push a lawn mower, cutting over 100 yards with quality—yes. A degree in Lawn Care Technology—not so much. If you start to focus your team member hiring search on degrees or certifications you are heading for poor team performance and as a bonus possibly acquiring a couple of pompous jerks who think they know everything.

College degrees do not mean today what they meant fifty years ago. In many cases they have simply devolved into a Human Resource hurdle to gain employment. For many people the four-year degree becomes the ticket to get interviewed, even if the skills learned at college couldn't also be learned by reading a few books. Typically, the answer comes back that at least it shows someone followed through and achieved a goal. This may be one of the worse excuses I have ever heard. To follow the logic, if a parent paid for a student to attend six years of college to attain the four-year degree, along with room and board as he searched for the easiest professors and planned his next party, are those the goal achievement you are looking for in a team member?

At one time you might have been able to make the case that a college degree demonstrated a person was pursuing knowledge and perhaps demonstrating a higher degree of intellect in a field. Whether that was ever the case is debatable and irrelevant. What is relevant is that most of today's typical college degrees do not translate into skills that can be used for the betterment of the team. A college degree has become more and more like a high school diploma was sixty years ago, something people attain for the sole purpose of acquiring a higher paying job. Anyone who thinks having any college degree pays more than having a high school diploma hasn't compared the pay of an office worker and a plumber. This scam is supported by colleges that are looking for more revenue, and if I am being charitable, a belief that somehow the degree is imparting skills that enable a person to contribute more to a team and society in general. The belief is also perpetuated by those of us with college degrees who want to believe having a degree matters more than any other requirement because, well, we have one. You could have spent four years becoming an alcoholic and barely passed "Exploring Psychological Expressions 201," but you have that all-important degree the team leader thinks is a "must have" to be successful.

If you also think someone must be "smart" to get a four-year degree you are not paying attention to the current state of "higher" education. If you think all professors are smart, you haven't attended a class in Guerrilla Theatre 102 or Pagan Rituals 302. The fact is that thousands of people who have no interest in higher education or critical thought are acquiring degrees. This includes many professors. It is turning into a high-priced, low-expectation gauntlet that enables people to secure the alleged golden ticket to improved employment opportunities. Even that statement can be challenged as more and more people secure degrees in a wide range of made-up degrees, a trend that has accelerated recently across academia. A degree may no longer be the golden ticket for some students that it was years ago, but it is gold in the bank for academia running this high-priced education scam.

Elite college degrees are no guarantee of finding excellent team members either. While I have met hard-working team members who went to an elite school, I have also met people who can pass a difficult exam on the latest theories in quantum physics but can't grasp fundamental concepts of working on a team to solve a problem or even care to communicate with anyone. In addition, going to an elite school lends itself to some degree of entitlement. Send these clowns to the competition. If I gave you the choice of having a Bill Gates, Sam Walton, or an Ivy League MBA with no experience setting up a team to be successful, who would you pick? Do you think that's a false choice? Open your eyes and check to see if your premise really holds up.

If the skills learned in a college environment are required for a new team member to be successful or enables an entry level person to come up to speed faster, then hire away. I suspect that when people make that claim many times there is a blind spot as it pertains to the term "college education." If you need an expert in Java software development, who would you hire?

- Candidate A: Emma has five years of development experience, but she dropped out of college to work full-time due to lack of money. She has developed several Java applications and knows how to deliver results.

- Candidate B: Jacob has a computer science degree and tells you what a go-getter he is. What Jacob isn't telling you is that he hates programming. His high school guidance counselor said he could get a high paying job if he got a computer science degree. Jacob took one class in Java at college and learned the right Java technical buzz words.

The other fun fact that is not on Jacob's resume? During that one Java class the professor spent seventy percent of the time ranting about politics instead of teaching Java software development. I suspect Jacob will also not divulge he couldn't have even passed that class if his girlfriend hadn't finished up his final project for him. Think about that as you tell Human Resources in the job description to require some type of four-year Computer Science degree as the condition of employment for this position. If two candidates possess the first three traits as well as communication skills, always hire the person with five years of experience and a proven track record. Leave that highly credentialed and entitled philosophy PhD at the local coffee house.

Certifications

Since college degrees are becoming common and the educational standards continue to decline, to speed up the hiring process teams have moved on to looking for additional certifications as a demonstration of the ability to work on a team effectively. Again, certifications should never trump the first three traits. In some cases, certifications may indicate the person has gained a certain proficiency of technical knowledge that you require. In other cases, you may be getting someone who expects something should be handed to them because they have five or six letters after their name. Passing a certification test means you passed a test. Do you really think that means a team member can apply the knowledge?

More than once, I was called in as part of a project clean-up team and discovered the certified project managers in charge could apparently pass a certification test but had to be removed from the team. They may have known how to build a complicated Project GANTT Chart, but they were terrible communicators and failed to implement the key concepts of leadership required to execute a successful large-scale implementation project.

What it comes down to is a certification becomes an indicator to Human Resources that you have the experience and know how to do the job. In the real world, for those of you that have experience hiring these types of alphabet soup candidates, you know that is not necessarily the case. Instead of working on improving the team many of them spend time working on adding more letters to their business card to make themselves more "marketable."

People driven by a desire for excellence and motivated by metrics are worth more than any expert at the high end of the market no matter how many letters are on their business card. What defines an expert? If you are letting certifications or degrees dictate the expert tag, you are just asking for aggressive expert behavior as discussed in Chapter 7. Let your competitors have all those overpriced certified experts who believe they are entitled because they passed a test. You are looking for smart people who demonstrate a commitment to excellence and have a proven track record. If something needs to be learned they will go learn it. If a new skill is needed, they will acquire it. If a team member needs help, they will lend a hand. This is worth more than any "know-it-all" who is a pampered, egotistical jerk. Why are certifications used in hiring? It is the safe path, and you won't be blamed if the new hire fails. After all, you hired someone certified so how could you know they were just certifiably lazy and unable to do the job?

Forget about titles, degrees, and fancy certifications. You are looking for smart people who are not afraid to get their hands dirty, have a work ethic, are goal oriented, and are motivated by financial and operational metrics. By that I mean motivated by money and doing a quality job. If they are too good to perform a task that needs to be done because they have a master's degree and the task is "beneath" their educational level, let the competition have them on their team. Focus on what the team needs to achieve its objectives. Ask your team members what they think is required to be successful. They are closest to the work. What are the metrics that will be applied? How will they be measured? Only then can you start the process of putting the job description together and what it takes to succeed.

STEP 2: FULFILL THE NEED

Congratulations, you now know what you need. It is time to go on the mission to recruit people to join your team. Warning: there are barbarians at the gate. They have one mission—to enter your village and pillage the town for their own self-serving needs. They will spend hours preparing whatever Trojan Horse is required to get through your fortified gate. How do you keep all of them out of your walled city? You can't. You can have one-hundred interviews, perform brain scans, and yet someone will still get in and cause damage. All you can do is minimize the number who get though and then make sure you have enough defenses on the inside, i.e., metric police, to dispatch any marauders.

TEAMWORK MOMENT OF TRUTH

You can't ensure the team member you are hiring isn't bad. You can only minimize the possibility and be prepared to correct your mistake.

Where do you begin? There are three buckets to choose from:

- Planet Your Team.

- Your Solar System.

- The Unknown Universe.

Planet Your Team

Within the larger organization there will be candidates who may fit your requirements. The good news is that you will have a good idea how they will meet your work ethic and goal achievement criteria. You also should have an idea of their technical skills as they won't be able to tell you they commanded a nuclear aircraft carrier in their last job when in fact they commanded the espresso machine downstairs. The bad news is that if the general organization doesn't have the same love of metrics and results that your team does there may be undue pressure from a variety of sources, including your boss and HR, that believe since a person has been there a while they deserve the position. If that is the case resist and move on to the next group! As discussed, you may also face the fact that HR, or your boss, is also biased against any current employees and dream of you hiring that mythical unicorn.

Your Solar System

Yes, your network. Those people you have worked with and who you know will produce the results you need. Warning, when I say network that doesn't mean your social media friends, your brother-in-law, or the guy at another company that bought you a beer at a conference. I wish the previous statement was unnecessary. Unfortunately, I have seen far too many of these types of hires by smart people, therefore I feel it is my fiduciary responsibility to tell you it is not a good idea. Interview only those who fit your requirements and will deliver results. Again, you must resist the powerful emotion to circumvent everything discussed in setting up requirements because you know someone who needs a job. The power of rationalization is strong. Even the strongest willed among us will be tempted at times to help a friend or family member. Searching the network means performing a high degree of self-analysis to remove emotional attachments as much as possible. If you can't resist hiring a friend or relative who is not qualified, do you think there is any chance you will be able to fire them if they turn out to be incompetent?

Everyone wants a tough, extensive hiring process until it's their nephew who needs a job. I have seen organizations that have all these HR rules and structures and processes in place and then a manager or executive wants their child hired and, boom, they're in. You have done serious long-term damage with that decision no matter how great your child is. They will never have credibility, your HR department trust will go to zero, and the entire process becomes corrupt. You have lost before you began. I understand that in some cases people will feel strongly that their family member or friend would be a good fit. In some cases, such as for an entry level position, there can be more flexibility. At the very least don't have them report into you if you really think they are good and could contribute to the team. This helps avoid losing your credibility with your employees while also enabling your family member to have a chance to prove they were an excellent hire and not just a welfare case forced on some poor manager because the executive ordered it. Consider yourself warned.

Now that I have given you the bad and the ugly, here's the good. When you have real work experience with people who meet the requirements of the position, you save time and help reduce the chances of having to let them go. If no one on your planet or in your solar system fits the requirements, including your unemployed brother-in law, it is time to boldly go where only fools tread. The unknown universe.

The Unknown Universe

Yes, the vast cold universe that contains many wonders as well as dangers. There are many candidates who in just a few months could turn your team into the greatest producing team in the history of the world. The only problem is there are even more candidates who will destroy everything you have built. You already know that the *cheval fumier* documentation will not really clear up the mysteries of the universe. The next step as you journey into deep space is to uncover as much as you can. Hopefully, you can find the stars that align with your mission and keep out the others. If you want to see the power of modern technology and have about three hundred hours a week available, go ahead and place an ad on an internet job site. You will be entertained for hours by:

- People who are unfamiliar with the spell check function.

- Applicants from other countries who are making a poor attempt at getting you to help them enter your country.

- People who are so lazy they can't even lie on a resume and send you their standard one that contains no experience related to the position you are hiring for.

- Salary shoppers with no intent of leaving whatever position they are in, and most of the time that is a good thing for you.

- People who make you question whether the human race has any hope

It is better that you narrow your search of the unknown universe to specific galaxies. Professional organizations or referrals from business associates you trust are a good place to start, along with members of the current team—no I don't mean recommend their spouse! This, of course, requires a serious amount of time and effort. After a while there is a tendency to give up and pick from the best two candidates you have right now, aka dumb and dumber. This is one of those few areas where outside help can do an effective job screening the candidates. If you are large enough to have an HR department that has people with this skill set, great. If not, you need to engage a respectable recruiter. While "respectable recruiter" may sound oxymoronic to some of you based on experience, there are many who would like repeat business and can be helpful as you attempt to screen out applicants.

THE INTERVIEW PROCESS

No matter where the candidate comes from, they should all go through the same process. The interview process should be at least a four-step approach.

- Introduction Interview.
- Team Leader Interview.
- Team Interview.
- Final Interview.

Introduction interview

A video or in-person interview can be conducted by HR during the screening process. If you don't have an HR person, or recruiting company you trust, the team leader can conduct a quick interview.

Using the appropriate questions at this step helps eliminate obvious issues-like work ethic, accountability, or signs of outright insanity. It also filters out candidates with glaring communication problems. A video interview is also effective at weeding out the drive-by resume crowd. Just a few questions will demonstrate they have absolutely no skill set associated with what you need on the team.

This doesn't mean you can delegate any part of the hiring process. If HR is doing the introduction interview don't expect them to be able determine if a person has the appropriate skills based on the resume. At best they might be able to eliminate the fry cook who is applying for the brain surgeon position. The key thing is there is way too much emphasis on technical skills and not enough on soft skills, because technical skills are easy. That means they may just be checking boxes such as what degree they have, certifications, jargon words, and how many years of experience. If all your recruiters are doing is looking at technical skills on a resume, you should fire them and have the front-line managers look at the résumés. It is understood that no matter the position you must have the rudimentary skills to do the job. The problem with this type of thinking is too many people hire based on that and whether the person doesn't come across as a jerk or is boring during the interview.

No matter what the hiring process is, the typical job interview process puts a premium on résumé points followed by a candidate's acting ability. Is it any wonder so many organizations end up hiring poor performers—despite their supposedly "great" processes?

Team manager interview

Now it is time for the first real interview after the initial screening. If you have a Human Resource department or recruiter doing the initial screening, remember there is a tendency for them to go for good actors and "rah rah" personalities no matter what the position. Hiring a software developer? Not required. Selling products over the phone? Perhaps. Your task is to formulate key questions around goals, work ethic, and working with others to achieve goals.

Don't ask questions such as do you like working on teams. Duh, your acting 101 candidate knows how to field that softball question. Here, write down the answer. I love working on teams. Teams can accomplish so much more than one person, blah, blah, blah. Instead, frame your questions around the characteristics of someone who will be successful on your team. Don't even mention the word team. Construct scenarios on how they would deal with certain situations. Probe their answers. Don't let them get away with formulated answers such as, "I would call the team together for a brainstorming session and come to a consensus." Stop them and ask what if there are no brains on the team to storm with? Look for dedication to excellence, to being the best goal-oriented person on the team.

When you are interviewing candidates, the goal is to move past the canned interview question and answer format. You need free-form discussion points. It also requires a high degree of listening skills. For example, you have asked them to describe a failed project they were on and provide some analysis as to why it failed. Make the interview a conversation as opposed to a monologue from you on what the job is about. Interrupt answers and ask clarifying questions. This tends to force a candidate off canned answers. If a person has never been on a failed project in any of the positions on their resume, I would question their integrity or connection with reality. Even if you are hiring an entry level position, at some point, they must have played on a losing soccer team or worked for a dysfunctional assistant manager at a local fast-food job.

The key thing is not to just ask the question like you are a government agent in the interrogation room. The suspect will continue to be on guard and secretly take their Fifth Amendment right to not incriminate themselves. The interview needs to become a conversion about work, their viewpoints, and approach. You must learn to interrupt politely and use part of their answer to launch into more probing questions; all centered on how they perform the work—not how much they like teamwork. You must also avoid talking too much about yourself or the company, no matter how awesome the interviewee says your company is and how excited they are to be considered.

A good candidate can talk forever about the awesome project they managed. When they can't answer what didn't work and how they learned from that experience is when you should get concerned. Some will simply refuse to engage and steer back to canned answers. This is a warning sign.

Do you have any questions for me?

This is a last standard question that hiring and recruiting books say is very important to determine if you have a good candidate. I always ask the question, but I don't ask it because I think it is critical in finding out more about the candidate. Real questions should occur during the interview if you are having a give and take conversation. If that is your one big question during an interview, suggest you cut back on the monologue and have a dialogue with the person.

I still ask the question because you never know what you are going to get, and sometimes it's downright entertaining. Years ago, I was interviewing a project manager who appeared highly qualified. He gave all the right answers and the interview was going smoothly.

Then I asked, "Do you have any questions for me?" "Why yes." He said, "Do I have to work hard here?" I was dumbstruck. I paused, and then asked, "What do you mean by work hard?" He replied," I have a lot of hobbies and I'm looking to achieve a balanced life. I want to make sure there won't be unnecessary demands on my time here. For example, I need to always leave work by 4:30PM."

Rarely do you get that level of honesty from a softball question. It was the moment I understood why books like "Interviewing for Complete Morons" exist. The flip side? Many candidates don't want to work—you just don't find out until after they're hired. I appreciated the honesty.

Questions to avoid

I suggest you avoid the following questions because they are not helpful, useless, or are just stupid when you give it some critical thought

The ambition interview question

Some interviewers are impressed when a candidate discusses where they want to be in ten years, because it shows ambition. I couldn't care less what anyone says they want to do in ten years. For all you know they will be a crack head living in a tent. You want someone who is focused on doing a great job at the job they are interviewing for today. When the interviewee says I want to be in senior management in ten years, watch out. This is usually a person dedicated to doing all they can to self-promote and everything else at the bare minimum. The only thing I care about is if their ambition is to be the best at the job they are interviewing for today. If they are that good the opportunities will come and one day I will report to them.

Until then, Skippy, how about starting out by just doing the job we hired you to do well?

The do-you-like-working-on-teams question

Seriously do I have to answer this?

Team Interview

While I know some team leaders think they are the team genius and can handle all the technical questions, you aren't, and if you are what kind of dolts did you already hire? As a leader, I prefer to have people know more than me in their area of expertise, because they are doing it every day. If you have a great team, it's time to trust that they don't want to let any résumé enhancers join who will create more work for the team-not help the team. Do they think the person has the right skill set to succeed in the position?

This is the interview where a person needs to "prove" they have the technical abilities to work on the team, as opposed to fooling the team leader, and how hard is that really? Work with your team to craft some technical questions to have a discussion. This should be a roundtable discussion with peers about the work. Some candidates may have been able to BS you with how they developed an application. It gets harder to razzle dazzle the actual team members they will work with. I have seen many candidates exposed by the team interview. Software development savant? Your development team can sniff out what they actually know as opposed to what they told you they know. Marketing guru? Your marketing team would like to hear the details of the concept the candidate developed and how they implemented it. A group of auto mechanics will cut through the BS quickly regarding experience working on cars.

Use the team. Remember they don't want any clowns joining the team either unless of course you are hiring for a circus. If the team approves and you hire the candidate, you are gaining something else: Faster acceptance and inclusion by the team. They were part of the process and will want the new employee to succeed. They will also help and mentor. Warning! Only use the team interview after you have a high-performing team in place. Otherwise ask yourself the following question:

Should I use a low performing team to perform an interview?
Answers:

A. Yes, because you are looking to dramatically improve your team and what better way than to ask a bunch of low performers who is the best qualified to show how bad they are in comparison.

B. No, because I have regained my common sense after years of team training brainwashed me into using teams to make all decisions. In some cases, there are team members who shouldn't be allowed to give directions to the restrooms.

Managers Outside the Department

Having areas that work closely with your team do an interview helps tremendously, especially if the team member will be working with that department in some manner. They don't know the details of the technical portion of the job, so they usually focus on the communications skills. If it is another department you work with, this also shows you value their opinion on a candidate.

Second-Level Manager Interview

If you are building a winning team and have hiring team managers reporting to you, I suggest they interview the candidate as well. This performs two important functions:

- It helps mentor your team managers on what matters most in the interview process as you view the top two or three candidates they are looking at.

- It is a double-check on allowing barbarians in the through the gate.

You have just increased you chances of hiring an excellent team member to 80 % by having feedback from each of these areas. If you get 100% thumbs-up the person is usually successful. The percentages go down from there. If you are the only one who thinks a candidate will be a good fit, check your premise. Maybe they have the same hobbies as you, which created a bias. Maybe you just clicked with their personality. The hardest thing to do as a team leader is to turn down a candidate who you think will work when everyone else says they won't. Remember, of course, this only pertains to high-performing teams you already have put in place that you trust. Never do this with teams that are low performing unless you want to hire more of that.

FINAL INTERVIEW

Lose Your Stereotypes

Before you start the interview process you must work very hard to lose your mental stereotypes. We discussed earlier some of the biases that come into the resume review process, such as graduating from an elite school or possessing alphabet certifications. There are also stereotypes and bias based on things such as sex, race, age, and color that you must weed out of the selection process. These are biases that do not readily appear during the résumés process but rear their ugly heads during the interview process. They must be weeded out for legal as well as moral reasons.

If you don't care about legal and moral reasons, how about a completely selfish team leader reason? If you let these biases affect you, you are limiting the talent pool and thus potentially leaving seriously talented people off the short list, people who could help your team. Your bias is also not supported by statistical evidence but is simply justified based on what you were taught at home, supported by other influences, and possibly a couple of personal experiences. Ask yourself when considering a candidate if you are allowing your person bias to influence your decisions. While there are areas of discrimination that you must force yourself to confront, there are other more subtle forms of discrimination that may impact your hiring decisions as well.

Generational discrimination

We're constantly bombarded in the media regarding the differences in generations in terms of consumer behavior, outlook on life, and what motivates the various generations. As if individuals can be segmented so easily. Specifically, the topic de jour is always the latest generation entering the work force. The conventional wisdom is they are different from any generation in history and teams must adapt the workplace to fit their requirements. This is rubbish. There has not been a time in human history where the older generation didn't think the next generation wasn't spoiled, more demanding, or had less of a work ethic. Conversely, has there ever been a time in human history where a twenty-two-year-old didn't feel constrained by the traditions and attitudes of the older generations? It's called being young.

TEAMWORK MOMENT OF TRUTH

There is no correlation between a good team player and what generation a person belongs to. There is a correlation between believing in age stereotyping and intellectual laziness.

Most people's idea of history is their own life mixed with some historical facts retained from school such as there was a Civil War and George Washington was the first president of the United States. Historical knowledge is all downhill from there. The fact is there were many lazy, incompetent, short-attention-span young adults in previous generations. In the 1950s they didn't have video game slackers— they called them beach bums. In the sixties they were called hippies. Five thousand years of recorded history shows that if you lower expectations of people you get lower results. Stop doing that to the younger generations. Demand excellence and reward accordingly. Didn't their parents ruin them enough? In the interview make sure they know that not everyone will get a soccer trophy at the end of the season.

There are good reasons we make excuses for young people entering the workplace. It validates your poor hiring and work decisions. Maybe it also validates your poor parenting that gave them such a high opinion of themselves. Even if you assume, and I disagree with this assumption, that they are different because they use social media apps and are not interested in working, then your job should be to find the 40% who still have the skills required to succeed. Let your competition waste time training their staff on programs to entice the other 60% of young people who don't think that work is important to come to work for them.

"Seasoned" employees

Conversely there are some who look at only the young as motivated, energetic, and open to new ideas. If you mean new ideas like beer bong parties, just remember that new ideas don't necessarily mean good ideas. There is the canard of the young go-getter being preferable to the seasoned employee stuck in his or her ways. In my thirty years of working in organizations hiring and firing people, I find this is more of a myth than ever. Driven by popular media it has entered the realm of accepted gospel even among team executives who should know better. The only evidence that appears to support this belief is that new team members are more positive about the company they work for. The only reason for that is they haven't been around long enough to understand how poorly run your team is. Give them five years and they will be just as unmotivated as every other generation that is working for you.

It is interesting how some classify work ethic based on age. At age twenty a person is ambitious when they work 60 hours; at age forty they are considered workaholics. Another interesting factor is the myth of older team players taking more time off due to illness. For those of us in the real world of teams, young workers also have a tendency of not showing up to work as well. In addition to the potential for illness, they are more likely to be out for other legitimate reasons, such as their child being sick. There are also the not-so-legitimate reasons such as partying late into the night, and personal "issues" including girlfriend and boyfriend dramas. This all contributes to time off for younger employees. Think back, that includes all of you in the older generations when you were young.

We are also so typically locked into our own world view about generational differences that we are convinced there are huge differences in generations when it comes to work ethic and ability to contribute. The effects of social media and the constant attempt at segmenting humans into categories have intensified. The differences are sometimes just on the surface. Just like any other time in history, each generation brings a unique perspective. Instead of segmenting people into age groups and stereotyping them we should all try to appreciate and value the perspective every individual brings to the team. I have a news flash: Whatever generation you are from your music was not the "best ever." Just because you listened to twenty songs over and over again during the good old days doesn't mean they were the best. There are great artists and music from every generation; there was music in your era that really sucked. That goes for people too. Take off your blinders

I Need Another Me

As a team leader maybe you've become convinced of your brilliance because you were bestowed the title of leader. From this comes a new definition of a team player: A person who agrees with all your brilliant ideas instead of questioning them. It is also a person that has your same personality or simply someone you can relate to.

What you need isn't you. You already have you. You need them. A department "groupthink" team will have a difficult time adjusting to new ideas, new methods, and solving problems. You can't find anyone like you. You can find plenty of people who will act like you if it looks like you want that. Typically, the only thing getting another you will accomplish is feed your ego.

All these traits are actual biases that are not based in fact any more than discriminating against people by race or religion. You are leaving valuable candidates off the table because of your own false perception of the world. Focus on what you need to succeed.

HEDGING AGAINST MISTAKES: PROBATION PERIOD

So, you've hired a good team member, or so you think. The first thing you need to recognize is that no matter what you do you will make a mistake and hire a bad team member (or two). Some people have practiced the art of getting a job for years and know exactly what to say to an HR person to get through the door and then convince you they are the best candidate. It doesn't matter how long you interview, how you interview, what battery of tests you put a candidate through. Six months later you are questioning your sanity. How did I ever hire this loser? Guess what; you will hire a loser. It is what you do about it when that revelation comes to you that matters.

Every person should start at a company on probation. This should be stated upfront as well as how at any time in the process they are subject to dismissal without cause. This needs to be used effectively. At minimum there should be a 90-day probation period subject to another 90 days if the person has not had enough time to demonstrate capabilities. Many teams have this policy on paper but many team leaders don't use it effectively. If a person is told upfront if you have the work ethic, the skills, and want to accept accountability and responsibility, probation should not be a worry. This is why it is important to make sure they understand the metrics BEFORE accepting the position.

Yes, some will slip through the cracks. The good news is you can effectively eliminate most of your problems by taking the time upfront to keep many of the idiots outside the door. Probation should help eliminate most of your remaining poor hiring decisions if used effectively. Did I mention that no matter how good you are at hiring people, occasionally you will fail, and fail miserably?

I hired a project manager a few years ago who appeared to have all the right qualities. He said all the right things in the interviews and his résumé looked great. He was even certified, so what could possibly go wrong? There was only one problem—it turned out he was incapable of managing a project or clients. How could this be? He was a certified "Project Manager Professional," had an extensive résumé, had gone to a good school, and had all the right answers to my questions. As a bonus I discovered he also had no organizational skills, refused to ever take accountability, and had no work ethic. When he was let go, he was in disbelief. He stated he had never been fired before. Well, this must be your lucky day. Consider this a learning experience and your opportunity to "grow" — somewhere else. Your probation is revoked. I wanted to tell him I was also in disbelief that I hired such an awful project manager and will consider this a learning experience as well on the next hire.

TEAMWORK MOMENT OF TRUTH

No matter what the process, how long you take, how many interviews they go through, what books you read on hiring, or how smart you are, you will occasionally hire an idiot.

Hiring is no different from every other team concept. Anyone who has read any books or taken any classes knows you must keep the inept, the stupid, the incompetent, the psychotic, and the general non-performers off the team. You must also ask the right questions and know what you really need. If we "know" this than why do we keep opening the door, allowing them to move in and stay on the team forever? The same reason we avoid every other fundamental concept of creating effective teams. It takes time and is hard work. Why work hard when the consultant told me I can have a 30% "lift" in quality hires by implementing their best-in-class hiring decision element software along with management training? Just remember, putting up with bad behavior for years is hard work too.

Now you have a great team that understands the financial and operational metrics that are needed to succeed. You also have a solid plan on how to add additional members to the team when needed and who will fit in with the metrics and culture you are building. Unfortunately, this isn't a math problem and once solved you have the answer for ongoing success. A leader's work is never completed. It moves and changes based on the situation at hand. How do you maintain the momentum with your high-performing team?

CHAPTER 13

TAKING IT TO THE NEXT LEVEL

"I do not believe in a fate that falls on men however they act; but I do believe in a fate that falls on them unless they act."

BUDDHA

O ne of the cheapest and easiest things to say is, 'we have to take it to the next level.' I have heard that countless times in business meetings, discussions, and strategy planning sessions. How do you take it the next level? What is the next level? Level of what? The only level that most are striving for is the next level of blather. Blather that is undecipherable by design to achieve the appearance of wanting to get something done.

If you are not in this category, then before you answer these questions you must ask yourself a more fundamental question. Are you ready to stop your search for the quick and easy answers to your organizational problems? Are you ready to stop the insane and elusive quest for synergy? A term that is representative of all the false gods we fall in love with thinking they will lead us to salvation. Yes, it is an illusion. There is no synergy, just people doing work. Some will do it well, others not so well. No amount of training, leadership retreats, bribes, or general pleading will change that.

> ## TEAMWORK MOMENT OF TRUTH
>
> You don't need to take it to the next level. You need to take it to THE level. The level of individual excellence.

THE PATHS TO FIX TEAMWORK PROBLEMS

How do you get to the level of individual excellence? There are three paths that team leaders usually employ to fix their teamwork problems:

- Cheap and easy.
- Expensive and easy.
- Expensive and hard.

Each of these paths usually have the same outcome.

Cheap and Easy

If you take a group of humans in a dysfunctional environment and send them to a seminar or training, you will get an amazing result. Your team will transform into group of humans in a dysfunctional environment, but now with certificates in hand that they completed a team program. If you do this training enough times, it is no longer as cheap. It is also never as cheap as you think it is when you account for the time away from doing the job you allegedly hired people to do. Of course, how many teams really factor in opportunity costs when they send team members away? Since you are paying them anyway, why not send them to even more training since it really doesn't cost any "real" money? In some cases, sending dysfunctional team members to training does help since it enables the rest of the team to finally get something done. The "good" news is since there is no way to track opportunity cost on your team it doesn't enter the cost/ benefit analysis to begin with.

Since team training has been tried at least five million seven-hundred fifty-thousand times without any evidence of long-term gain, why do people keep trying it? If you eliminate the clinically insane, the remaining team leaders will continue the charade because everyone is invested in this game working. The seminar provider needs the money; the team leader needs a solution that shows something is being done about the team problem. The team leader then needs to prove it worked to justify the cost and show the idea wasn't a waste of time. How is it proven? A survey of the participants is the usual method, and since everyone rates the training an 8 out of 10, it is declared a success. Good luck trying to apply any actual financial or operational metrics to this boondoggle. The good news is because it was cheap no one usually spends much time questioning whether it worked.

Expensive and Easy

If cheap and easy doesn't work, how about taking it to the next level—expensive and easy? The key here is that easy continues to trump other requirements such as critical thought when addressing team performance. All you need to do is click here on:

Ihavetheholygrailforteamperformancetool.com

You will be amazed at the presentation slides full of animation and complicated human resource interaction tools that will be at your disposal. Just sign the contract and watch magic happen. At that point you have only two outcomes. The application is installed with no customization and ignored, thereby keeping it expensive and easy with minimal effort from your team. Or there is a more likely outcome—expensive and hard.

Expensive and Hard

You bought IT and now by God you are going to make people use IT. Right after of course the customization for your "unique" environment that can't be replicated anywhere else in the galaxy so the functionality must be included on the advertised out-of-the-box system. The only unique thing about your methodology is the extent of its dysfunctionality. On top of expensive and hard this will also be complicated. The results are in, and we know that implementing an enterprise-wide collaborative software program is definitely hard work.

The business analysis, the software coding, the computer hardware implementation, training, and process changes require thousands of hours of very hard work by very dedicated people. The question becomes: Did you perform the right hard work? Hard work translates into necessary work in the eyes of those team members who are performing it. If you then begin to question "necessary" work, you will quickly become the enemy that must be neutralized. They have thousands of white papers and spreadsheets "proving" all the soft-cost savings gains. They also can fall back on conventional wisdom and the fact that executives read all the same articles and website stories you do. In addition, how many vendors and methodology consultants will help you form a business case that their solutions aren't necessary?

One of the most useful aspects of organizational behavior is that the more complex the technology solution the easier it is to blame failure on implementation problems or training issues. This means if you propose a massive, overly expensive "solution" there is the possibility that it will fail, and you will escape unscathed from an accountability perspective.

Most of your management team knows this is going to be a boondoggle. They also know that a senior team leader has invested an enormous amount of personal capital into this project and will shoot the first person who objects. Your team also knows after years of experience that if you raise objections, you obviously were not supporting the implementation so therefore are part of the problem. It is best to wait for the crash and then everyone can join in to claim it was an implementation issue. If you really want to drill down there were communication problems, the vendor lied about the product and minimized the level of effort needed, and the entire team did not fully support the initiative. All these reasons are true. They mask the overriding problem, which is no solution was ever going to work as the marketing bullet points said it would because your team sucks.

Against this large army on your side is just, well, you. There might be a rag-tag guerrilla army of supporters or a secret society on the team. Unless you can determine what the secret handshake is, no one will fess up. The only thing you have on your side is an appreciation of 5,000 years of recorded human history, and understanding of human behavior, and a positive cynical view of human motivations and actions. Once you have recognized cheap and easy or hard and expensive are false choices you can proceed with the steps necessary to be successful. You can now overcome the objections to real change that leads to real teamwork and create a new plan. In other words, cheap and hard!

TEAMWORK MOMENT OF TRUTH

Taking teamwork to the next level does not mean spending money on training, tools, and methodologies. It means spending time on individuals and metrics.

THE REAL SOLUTION: CHEAP AND HARD

You can achieve great teamwork in your organization, and you don't need even one seminar on teamwork to do it. What you need are great individuals who will in turn make a great team. You can now cancel that order for the $1 million collaborative project software and implementation boondoggle. The good news is that humans will always figure out how to work together when their individual needs and objectives are aligned with the team. The bad news is that in most modern organizations people have lost sight of these simple concepts in favor of implementing complex "solutions" that provide no real long-term benefits—at least none to the team.

All too often complex is confused with sophisticated and smart. It enables everyone to believe they are doing something to improve teamwork and make the organization successful as if they were making incredible advances in science and engineering. How much smarter do we feel if we convince ourselves that along with all the technological advances, we have also advanced as humans and we've created magical synergy as opposed to just getting the new work done?

Why do we keep going for cheap and easy or hard and complicated? It comes down to a belief that complicated is viewed as smart and we hope that the next big thing will solve our problems without having to do the real hard work as leaders. By that I don't mean sending the team members off to perform hard work implementing your insane ideas on team improvement. Hard analysis work on your part is necessary to determine what makes up a successful team and how you need to improve it. Yes, I said you need to improve it, not "them."

What we have really achieved is sinking to the depths of organizational team dysfunctionality. When a particular team manages to achieve an objective, we think there must have been some kind of divine intervention bestowing synergy to the common folk. In other words, a blind squirrel does indeed find a nut sometimes. We immediately alert various schools of business that the Holy Grail has at last been found. Our hopes are once again dashed after the universal team methodology is implemented somewhere else and they don't see the same results. We then perform a postmortem analysis and determine that the program wasn't implemented fully or it lacked executive "buy in." This rationalization works until we discover the same team that saw all those great results one year is a complete failure the next.

Is it really a methodology problem, a people problem, or a leadership problem? Here's what it really is: time for you to raise the bar with each of the individuals on your team. It may look different, but work is still work whether it is building Stonehenge or a Space Station. Instead of wishing for magical fairy dust everyone should strive for plain old team success in reaching realistic and measurable goals and objectives that translate into what really defines success. That means achieving real operational and financial goals. To reach these goals requires everyone to understand their role and their metrics for success.

This doesn't mean spending millions of dollars for complicated tools and methodologies. It also doesn't mean you are required to hire the high priest and priestess that have come down from the mountain, i.e., training consultants, to bestow their wisdom on the common dolts. I know; how boring is that when I can install a collaboration app on your team's smart phones that integrates with the cloud. I can then brag about it to the CEO, who is not very technically savvy, and so thinks you are a tech savant. While some of these solutions appear to help teams make money, typically they are a short-term façade that can't be backed by any financial or operational analytics that can be construed as meaningful to determining the overall performance of the team. Yes, you might say you lowered costs on team A. You usually just transferred the cost to Team B, or diluted the cost across team B through Z.

You can always spot an organization in trouble when they are attempting to deal with team performance issues by applying software, copyrighted breakthrough process methodologies, extensive training in team skills, and executive retreats to build teamwork. Of course, everyone says it was a great experience and will help. It will also change nothing if the fundamental concepts presented in this book regarding metrics and accountability are not enforced. Two months later, other than having the teamwork book on the shelf, there is no evidence that anything has been implemented.

You have not addressed the fundamental problems either with you own actions or the metrics that drive each individual's behavior. Process automation to improve the "team" should be looked at with extreme skepticism. There are powerful forces at work driving the view that process automation equals better performance. In jobs requiring human interaction the evidence of this helping an organization take it to the next level are sketchy at best. What isn't debatable is how much real dollars you are committing to get the alleged soft cost benefits of collaborative software implementations. The fact is that if you have a dysfunctional team before the software is installed, you will have a dysfunctional team afterward, and now it will include all the new dysfunctional technical experts you hired to maintain the system. This is true even after someone recommends you can improve it by putting the application in the "cloud".

TEAMWORK MOMENT OF TRUTH

Your complicated methodology to get teamwork done is a complicated mythology.

Complicated methodologies that are really dressed-up simple methodologies waste time and effort. Following are two different approaches to determine how to proceed on a product idea:

PRODUCT PROCESS METHODOLOGY APPROACH 1

Idea → Analysis → Go/No Decision → Develop

PRODUCT PROCESS METHODOLOGY APPROACH 2

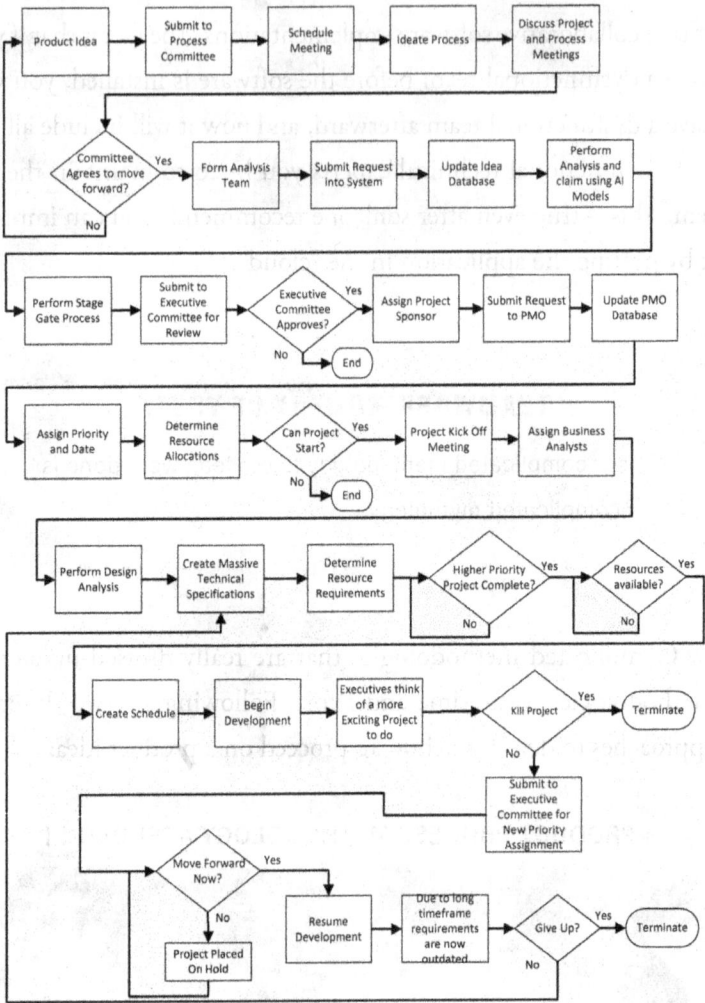

There is not one difference between the two, other than you spent months 'brainstorming the process' followed by 80 hours creating the complicated diagram that appears to correspond with the complicated project initiation process you developed. In fact, you have just dressed up the simple with the complex, thus ensuring long-term failure.

There are a couple of other points you must recognize as you start on your journey to take it to the next level. No matter how many hours you put into the work, you will have to constantly recalibrate. There are many great ideas about organizations, management philosophies, and theories. I encourage you to continue to read about them. Some may even help you. However, no matter what you do the only guarantee in team management is that at some point:

- Teams will fail.
- Individuals will fail.
- You will fail.

Since we have applied technology to make things more complex to continue make things faster and cheaper, why not make human interaction faster and cheaper? Because making human interaction more complex ignores the basic human model. Humans are not computers and are unpredictable. They change and arrive at the creative process differently. While machines can be upgraded overnight the human mind is a slowly evolving organism. When you go back just five revisions, or in software tech speak iterations, of humans, that takes you back to someone who may remember the 1700s. This means that human culture, our native intelligence, methods of communicating with each other, and personality types are not all that different from 200-plus years ago.

While humans now have "smart" phones, we haven't made humans smarter by having one. What we have done is enable humans to move from being entertained by minstrels on the street to watching them on a 6-inch screen at work. Technology may be changing the world from a tactical perspective, but it is not changing core human nature. Our narrow vision spans only what we know, which is our short lifetime. We then think we are different because we can "tweet" short messages on social media. They tweeted in 1530 as well. They just used birds to deliver short messages tied to their leg, and the birds did, in fact, tweet.

TEAMWORK MOMENT OF TRUTH

Confusing technology and process innovation with teamwork results in team failure.

Accept that humans have not changed a great deal in three thousand years. We haven't gotten smarter either. What we have done is built upon our knowledge of the physical world and our understanding of complex mathematical equations. Well, actually, I should say that a small subset of the human population now has a deeper understanding of complex mathematical equations and application to science and technological advancement. In the process we have discovered how to create more complex "things." Our error is mistaking this increased technical knowledge and ability to build complex things with our own human intelligence evolution.

Humans only know more about things. By applying the fundamental skills of motivation that have been part of motivation techniques for more than three thousand years, you can take it to the next level. While your competitors are spending millions to find the answer to their workforce team problem you have discovered there is no workforce team problem. There is just a workforce. The same workforce that people have dealt with for five thousand years. Longer if you count the caveman who was too lazy to go on the hunt and pretended to be sick. The same attitudes, misanthropic behavior, psychotic, high IQ, sense of entitlement, dumb, hardworking, lazy workforce that has always been with us.

The reason emperors terrorized their subjects was because it worked. Maybe not over the long term, but that was never the objective. Societies that are open to the possibility of human freedom and encourage individual creativity and achievement are more likely to advance the human condition. Innovation does not occur when the boss orders humans to be innovative, or create an "innovation process, or worse "ideate"; a buzzword that should make your head hurt. Provide the goals and objectives; then hire the right individual performers for the team. When it comes to performance you need to take it to THE level. The level of excellence. Then, no matter what new functions, actions, products, or technology comes your way, you have the methodology to put a team together to meet the challenge.

TEAMWORK MOMENT OF TRUTH

You can only take it to the next level by recognizing that humans in general have not taken it to the next level.

You have the keys to kingdom. The question is, are you willing to act? Everything in this book is easy to understand yet is hard work. Teams are like projects. No matter how bad the project goes everyone says we need to communicate better next time and then nothing changes. Teamwork in organizations is no exception. You have an incredible opportunity in front of you. Your competitors are adding millions of dollars in cost to incorporate expensive methodologies and hundreds of programmers building the holy grail of CRM systems employing a litany of high-priced consultants. Apply technology where it makes sense AFTER you have the right team in place.

You remove cost by instructing your leaders to lead and hold them accountable to lead. Require everyone in the organization to be autodidacts, close the high school or romper room kindergarten teams and get busy. If an executive doesn't know how to set up a great organization, why are they employed on your team? Do your team leaders put their faith in long-term employees, friends, or a misplaced belief in the power of technology to fix a people problem? Do they believe that everyone will work hard if you take the time to find out what motivates them? Do you have time to figure that out? Leave that to the employee's therapist. If they are not motivated, find someone who is. It's easier and cheaper despite what studies purport to show.

Were the team members or leaders promoted for social reasons, their level of incompetency, or because of their technical knowledge? You have some hard decisions to make and will likely hurt the feelings of people who were loyal. The harsh reality is many of these so-called loyal people were never acting in your team's best interest to begin with. They were using you and the organization to achieve their individual ends, just like everyone else, and they were not aligned to your vision. You must make the changes starting now.

In doing so you will reach a level of performance that your competitors will have a hard time matching. The unshakeable conventional wisdom is that team success is only achieved with more technology and/or outside methodology consulting, so many will consider you some sort of technological troglodyte who is unable to see the clear path to success. Be strong and laugh at them. They have a slide presentation with thousands of "data points." You have thousands of years of human history on your side. It is time to make the choice to finally improve your team. It all comes down to the final teamwork moment of truth.

THE LAST TEAMWORK MOMENT OF TRUTH

At the end of the day, you will have to choose individual greatness and hard work or place your faith in Synergy and putting "There is no I in Team" on coffee mugs.

THE CHOICE IS YOURS...

NOW, GO TEAM!

ACKNOWLEDGMENTS

This book would never have crossed the finish line without the advice, encouragement, and unwavering support of my incredible team.

First and foremost, I want to thank my wife, Donna, whose steady encouragement over the years has helped me stay focused and reach my goals. I'm also deeply grateful to my daughter, Annalise Lynch, for her thoughtful input, draft editing, and ongoing support. To my daughters Cynthia, Jennifer, and Rachel—thank you for your encouragement and belief in me. I'm proud to be part of such an amazing family team.

Special thanks to my copy editor, Dennis Kouba, for his keen eye and guidance, and to Steve Kuhn for his creative work on the book cover and formatting design.

Beyond the core team, I owe a nod to the many people who cheered me on—sometimes with guilt-inducing remarks like, "Hey Jack, did you finish that book yet?" or my personal favorite, "Really? You're still working on that?" I would like to acknowledge every person who contributed to my guilt—and in a small way helped motivate me to finish this work. Emphasis on the word **small**.

ABOUT THE AUTHOR

From restaurant kitchens to executive leadership, Jack Lynch has experienced the full spectrum of team dynamics. His career spans decades of hands-on leadership roles, culminating in his role as Chief Risk Officer and President of a subsidiary, where he successfully led a multi-million-dollar fraud and risk operations unit across multiple office locations and virtual teams.

Jack's journey through teamwork is as diverse as it is deep—covering roles in construction, factory work, full-time musicianship, financial services, and technology. As a project manager at a Fortune 500 company, he spearheaded nationwide implementations and product development initiatives, consistently delivering results across complex, high-stakes environments.

He holds an Associate of Applied Science in Electronic Technology, a Bachelor's and Master's degrees in Business Management, and a Master's Certificate in Project Management.

A dynamic and engaging public speaker, Jack has also presented at numerous conferences and served on multiple advisory boards and working groups.

To inquire about Jack speaking at your event, visit

OWLPENGUIN.NET

or email info@owlpenguin.net

IMAGE CREDITS

www.ingramcontent.com/pod-product-compliance
Lightning Source LLC
Chambersburg PA
CBHW071548210326
41597CB00019B/3164